Disability as a Social Construct

DISABILITY AS A SOCIAL CONSTRUCT

Legislative Roots

CLAIRE H. LIACHOWITZ

UNIVERSITY OF PENNSYLVANIA PRESS

Philadelphia

Library of Congress Cataloging-in-Publication Data

Liachowitz, Claire H.
  Disability as a social construct : legislative roots / Claire H.
Liachowitz.
    p. cm.
  Revision of thesis (Ph.D.)—Bryn Mawr College.
  Bibliography: p.
  Includes index.
  ISBN 0–8122–8134–9
  1. Physically handicapped—Legal status, laws, etc.—United
States—History.   2. Physically handicapped—Legal status, laws,
etc.—Pennsylvania—History.   3. Physically handicapped—United
States—History.   4. Physically handicapped—Pennsylvania—History.
5. Sociological jurisprudence.   I. Title.
KF480.L53   1988
346.7301'3—dc19
[347.30613]   88–17153
                                                                    CIP

CONTENTS

This book is dedicated to
the memory of my parents—
the first people who taught me the importance
of respecting individual differences.

ACKNOWLEDGMENTS

An earlier version of this book was written as a doctoral dissertation at Bryn Mawr College. I thank Dean Phyllis Bober, Dean Barbara Kreutz, my faculty committee, and especially Professor Marc Howard Ross, for their long years of patience, encouragement and direction. I cannot come close to thanking adequately the remarkable people who staff the college library.

With the helpful criticism of caring friends and colleagues, the dissertation became a book. I am particularly grateful to Dr. Phyllis Forman, Tia Melaville, Dr. Andrea Boxer, Professor Judith Porter, Professor William Rossky, Dr. Bernard Graney, and Dr. David B. Schwartz.

PREFACE

At the time that Benjamin Franklin was chosen to represent Pennsylvania in the Constitutional Convention of 1787, he was almost immobilized by gouty arthritis, and Philadelphia's officials arranged to have him carried into the sessions in a sedan chair.[1] His physically defective body thus did not impede his ability to function as a statesman; although the impairment that prevented his walking remained, he was not disabled.

Franklin's experience illustrates the distinction between a handicap imposed by nature and a handicap imposed by society. This book expands on that distinction to show the ways that socially imposed handicaps have been constructed. The historical analysis that is used indicates that much of the inability to function that characterizes physically impaired people is an outcome of political and social decisions rather than medical limitations. The purpose of the present book is not to prescribe policy, although inquiry into the nature of disability clearly establishes a foundation for the kind of public policy that is not disabling—or better, that is "enabling."

The frequently debated question whether "disabled" or "handicapped" better describes people with limited bodily functions appears to me to represent little more than an issue of semantics so long as one of these terms refers to the functional limitations imposed by social environments. Completely arbitrarily, therefore, I have used the term "handicap" to indicate physical impairment and "disability" to indicate a diminished ability to function socially.

Literally, the words "physically handicapped" can describe persons with various forms of perceptual disorders or intellectual deficiencies. The term is also applied to persons with defective vision or hearing or with medical problems that are imperceptible to others. The conventional usage of "physically handicapped" of course refers to people with visible neuromuscular or orthopedic abnormalities. Throughout, I have used that customary definition, although some quotations focus on mental retardation and blindness. Even though I have largely dealt with a particular group of handicapped people, it is understood that *any* person who is believed to deviate from culturally acceptable physical norms is "physically handicapped."

Notes

1. Catherine Drinker Bowen. *Miracle at Philadelphia: The Story of the Constitutional Convention*, pp. 34, 254.

CHAPTER 1

Introduction

Until recently, most writers on the social aspects of physical handicap have adhered to the orthodox medical view of disability as the direct result of personal physical disorder. Now, in contrast, an increasing number of sociological and psychological theorists regard disability as a complex of constraints that the ablebodied population imposes on the behavior of physically impaired people.

This book looks at these limitations of function from a somewhat different perspective—not as the consequences of interpersonal relationships, but as the products of public, collective actions. Without a conception of disability as a social construct,[1] explanations of the results of modern "disability legislation" are incomplete. What is not accounted for is the fact that laws that deal with handicapped people reflect not only the political problems posed by conflicting interest groups, but also the views that biological deficiency confers social deficiency and that handicapped people deserve (perhaps desire) a place outside of the mainstream of society. Furthermore, useful legislative evaluations need to take into account the processes by which people who deviate from accepted physical norms are devaluated and segregated and, as a result, disabled.

The growth of these ideas is demonstrated here by analyzing laws and public documents that were developed prior to the early twentieth century. These early records suggest that the cultural practice of translating physical abnormality into social inferiority is so deeply rooted as to have had an almost certain impact on both the formulation and implementation of later public policy. Of course one cannot proclaim with certainty that values institutionalized over time have continued to shape subsequent public actions. However, the historical analysis so strongly supports such a relationship that it seems vital to consider this fact in the analysis of later legislation, and to apply it as a source of information for the formulation of new "enabling" legislation.

The book is based on the assumption that disability exemplifies a continuous relationship between physically impaired individuals and their social environments, so that they are disabled at some times and under some conditions, and able to function as ordinary citizens at other times and conditions. This point is supported by Barrington Moore's discussion of the causes of human misery. In a general theory that helps to explain the variable meanings that a society gives to the costs of caring for dependent people, Moore states that a cost must always be examined as a *cost for whom*.[2] His simple reminder makes sense of the idea of looking at disability in a political and social context.

Examining the laws that deal with physically handicapped people is a useful way to understand disability as a social creation, for the formal response of legislation reflects not only a history of what society defines as problems, but also a history of how laws have affected and shaped those problems. It will become clear that attitudes about human physical difference are but one determinant of these laws, and that neither a purely psychological nor a purely sociological approach can be used to explain the processes or the consequences of constructing disability. But analyzing legislation seems to be an effective approach to this methodological problem too, for public decisions disclose points at which individual and societal attitudes and behaviors affect one another.

Increasingly, as the frequent quotation of the following statement by Howard Becker indicates, sociologists look not at the person of the deviator but at the process of deviance:

> [S]ocial groups create deviance by making the rules whose infraction constitutes deviance, and by applying these rules to particular people and labeling them as outsiders. From this point of view, deviance is *not* a quality of the act the person commits, but rather a consequence of the application by others of rules and sanctions to an "offender." The deviant is one to whom that label has successfully been applied; deviant behavior is behavior that people so label.[3]

In accordance with the prevailing thought that deviance is a relativistic concept, modern labeling theory[4] attempts to explain a process; it does not focus on the characteristics of the deviator. Nevertheless, the kind of research that investigates the *reactions* to "deviance the status" can help to achieve an understanding of "deviance the process." Indeed, we will see in subsequent chapters many connections between responses by (and to) the deviator and the construction of disability. Although one important goal of the book is to specify these responses, its larger purpose is to demonstrate how particular laws have converted physical deviation into social and civil disability.

Bogdan and Taylor's discussion of the phrase "mental retardation" helps to establish the theoretical background for this purpose by clarifying the meaning of "social construction":

> As a concept, mental retardation exists in the minds of those who use it as a term to describe the cognitive states of other people. It is a reification—a socially created category which is assumed to have an existence independent of its creators' minds.[5]

Similarly, in *The Making of Blind Men,* Robert Scott shows that society shapes the identity and self-perception of blind people. He discusses the preconceptions and expectations that often characterize "workers for the blind"; he describes agencies that aim to serve people who are blind; he reports interviews both with "clients" and with blind people who have no relationship to formal agencies. The data that Scott collects permit him to conclude that blind people are *made*—that they are taught to behave in accordance with those expectations:

> The disability of blindness is a learned social role. The various attitudes and patterns of behavior that characterize people who are blind are not inherent in their condition but rather are acquired through ordinary processes of social learning. Thus there is nothing inherent in the condition of blindness that requires a person to be dependent, melancholy or helpless; nor is there anything about it that should lead him to become independent or assertive. Blind men are made, and by the same processes of socialization that have made us all.[6]

Scott's study emphasizes development of the sense of self more than this book does, and it does not focus in particular on the role of laws and their consequences in the creation of disability. Nevertheless, his conclusion that "blind men are made" is conceptually identical to the thesis that disability is constructed.

One way to make blind men is to teach them to believe the meanings of the labels that society attaches to them. This socializing mechanism can of course be generalized to any form of physical impairment, and has probably been most extensively discussed with regard to "I.Q. tests." For example, Sarason and Doris[7] write about the dangers to the individual of the "implicit and unverbalized assumptions" that accompany such testing. They make the crucial point that, although I.Q. tests are important diagnostic instruments, they are often thoughtlessly used to *explain* behavior. Their discussion is surely consistent with the argument that the labeling that accompanies this ostensibly innocent method of diagnosis can easily translate the method into one that justifies differential social treatment.

Another approach to understanding consequences of labeling is used by studies that compare interracial relationships to those between able-bodied and handicapped people. Apparently stimulated by Gordon Allport's classic study of prejudice,[8] several writers have used the concept of "stigma" to explain responses both to racial and physical differences.[9] Certainly there are clear similarities between members of the physically handicapped population and American blacks. First, most people who diverge from either racial or physical norms share the problem of evoking unpredictable, but usually negative, responses from the majority population. Second, whether based on biological ascription or social attribution, minority groups often face a common personal and political dilemma. Many of their members want the same treatment accorded those who meet culturally accepted norms, but think that they may need, and often construct their lives to rely on, the extraordinary treatment that society gives to an abnormal group. Third, members of both groups are often forced to meet their need for belonging, and their need for personal and political recognition, by establishing or joining groups composed "of their own kind."

Unlike persons whose skin color makes them members of a statistical minority, though, people with physical impairments comprise a group defined by the anatomical and physiological integrity of the human body. No reasonable evidence suggests that divergence from the norm of skin pigment affects integrity of the species. But even though the social position of members of each group is defined by society, the very existence of people who are physically different may engender perceptions of the fragility of both the human person and the human race. The fear stimulated by these perceptions may result in negative reactions to handicapped people. The work will show, though, that many factors other than feelings of fear cause disability.

Evidence in later chapters illustrates that definitions of disability vary with the purposes and intellectual disciplines of the definers. One of the several representations of disability as a social concept is contained in Eliot Friedson's "Disability as Social Deviance." Friedson defines a handicap as

an imputation of difference from others; more particularly, imputation of an *undesirable* difference. By definition then, a person said to be handicapped is so defined because he deviates from what he himself or others believe to be normal or appropriate.[10]

Among the many studies that support Friedson's thesis is a 1960 survey of Navaho health.[11] Responses to that survey indicate that these American Indians not merely allowed but expected their brothers and sisters with congenitally dislocated hips to perform within their society to the extent of their abilities. By that measure, these physically defective people did not deviate from the normal.

Friedson asserts that a handicap is socially constructed because it represents deviation from a socially valued norm. His definition, however, fails to account for questions of how this social creation comes about. In contrast to Friedson's declaration of cause and effect, this book argues that disability is a result of the various social constructions that *force* handicapped individuals into a position of deviance. One example of this process can be seen in the complex of problems of industrialization. Children who might have gotten along without difficulty with the elementary tasks of a farm may be unable to function well, or at all, under the demands of an industrialized city. Consequences of even minor physical impairments may thus be determined by socially created imperatives. A similar kind of process has been discussed extensively in the field of mental retardation where it is generally accepted that people who cannot meet the intellectual demands of school may nevertheless operate without difficulty in the world outside. The cause of these forms of dysfunction is not the derogatory label attached to an unacceptable difference, as Friedson's definition suggests. In these cases, the social situation itself forces an inability, or diminished ability, to function.

The concept of disability as forced deviation is in great part derived from C. Wright Mills' *The Sociological Imagination*[12] and Robert K. Merton's writings on anomie.[13] Although these works do not refer to the specific issue of physical impairment, their broad themes of societal enabling and disabling are consistent with the social model of disability. According to Mills and to Merton, the nature of personal functioning is often consequent to the status and labels that the majority society assigns to individuals. A number of recent writings by persons who deal with handicapped people also make this point. These studies question assumptions that social structures are unrelated to disability,[14] and that services of the rehabilitation professions are always and entirely helpful to their handicapped patients or clients.[15]

The several works of Wolf Wolfensberger,[16] for example, discuss the disability that is effected by the structures and persons of rehabilitation (or habilitation) systems. Although Wolfensberger's writings focus on how society deals with mentally retarded people who may or may not be physically handicapped in the sense used here, much of his analysis is pertinent to this book. His description of a desirable "management model" is in many ways consistent with the ideas advanced here, as is his statement that

> [M]ental retardation is well along to having overcome the fixation derived from the medical model . . . and has become management-oriented. This is not to say that etiology is not given adequate consideration in theory and research, but that management on the clinical level is no longer as preoccupied as formerly with etiological diagnosis.[17]

However, as his definition of "normalization" indicates, Wolfensberger's works differ in emphasis from this book:

> Utilization of means which are as culturally normative as possible, *in order to establish and/or maintain personal behaviors and characteristics which are as culturally normative* as possible.[18] [my emphasis].

Perhaps Wolfensberger is able to be prescriptive because of the extensive historical reviews of human care services that he and others have carefully developed. In contrast, this book only incidentally looks at implications for desirable policy. What is very different from the philosophy advanced here, however, is the fact that Wolfensberger's "normalization principle" focuses on adaptation *by* the individual who is considered to be deviant. Wolfensberger defines as deviant any person who is perceived to possess a major, negatively valued, difference. Presumably because of this view, he focuses on methods to prevent or reduce visible differences:

> [t]he probabilities should be minimized that a citizen can identify on sight, as being different, a person who is already deviant, or who is apt to be so labelled in the future.[19]

The emphasis in this book is not on the adaptation of the handicapped individual, nor on altering the norms of society so that the handicapped individual has the opportunity to adapt. The emphasis rather is on demonstrating the construction of disabling social norms, and on developing a perspective that suggests that *social structures and norms can and should adapt to the individual.*

But most views of disability conform only imperfectly to the idea of a social construct. For example, classical literary representations of handicapped people are almost invariably marked by the grossly stereotypical attributes of sin and evil and weakness.[20] Secondly, when the labels attached to handicapped people are systematically analyzed, little or no attention is paid to their relationships to the norms of an entire society. Instead, the labels are described, measured and explained by focusing on the attitudinal and behavioral reactions of ablebodied persons to those with physical impairments.[21] In addition, even though the simulations of social psychology may provide theoretical insights into the construction of disability, their data are usually derived from interactions of small numbers of individuals. Understanding connections between psychological responses and the process of lawmaking is undoubtedly important to a discussion of disability legislation. But one cannot generalize from observations of small groups to the analysis of the collective process of dealing with societal problems.

The comparative perspectives offered by most cross-cultural or cross-national studies also are not entirely congenial to the view advanced here. Generally, these studies are designed to identify the cultural factors that modify attitudes about physical abnormality,[22] not to explore the relationship between these attitudes and formalized collective policies.

Several recent American studies systematically inquire into the social determinants of disability. However, even though their narrow focus is empirically useful, these studies do not permit the more general argument that social institutionalization adds to the handicap of physical impairment. For example, individual studies discuss the history of vocational rehabilitation policy,[23] the development of Social Security Disability Insurance and the social class labels of its recipients,[24] contemporary judicial decisions,[25] employment opportunities,[26] experiments in independent living,[27] and problems of handicapped children.[28] These focused observations lead to useful bits of knowledge, but understanding disability as a social construction needs the direction of a more comprehensive perspective. A 1974 article by Thomas T. H. Wan[29] proposes a research model that seems based on such a view. Wan believes that disability should be studied as a product of three sets of factors. He identifies

1. agent factors—in language apparently inconsistent with his model, Wan calls these "disabling conditions" rather than physical impairments;

2. host factors—which he specifies as education, occupation, age, gender, and race; and

3. environmental factors—by which he means society's degree and pattern of industrialization, poverty and immigration.

This model offers the guidelines for this book.

Plan of the Book

This work looks at the handicapped population of America as it has been dealt with by laws, and thus reviews the nation's treatment of wounded soldiers, injured workers, handicapped adults, and physically impaired children. The four resulting chapters examine the process and the consequences of constructing disability by illuminating political sources of social devaluation, by demonstrating their incorporation into legislation and by suggesting mechanisms that translate legislation into social and civil inferiority. Although this examination is presented in separate chapters, the several arguments are not so neatly divisible and their development requires considerable repetition. This is especially apparent when the same law, The Vocational Rehabilitation Act of 1920, is considered in both Chapters 2 and 4. Each of these chapters, however, offers a perspective that permits different insights. From the point of view of realizing the democratic theory of equal opportunity, the Act of 1920 was a positive achievement, having expressed the decision that enabling physically handicapped people to participate in society was a proper function for the federal government. However, that piece of legislation bears another significant relationship to the promise of political equality—a relationship that exemplifies a major proposition of this book: some of the conceptions that informed that first federal rehabilitation act continue decades later to impose disability upon physically impaired people.

Coincidentally, the order of the chapters is chronological, for America's earliest expression of public concern was for wounded soldiers, and its most recent for handicapped children. But the sequence of chapters is intended to point out theoretically significant dimensions in the public treatment of handicapped Americans. As successive groups of handicapped people became objects of government concern, one can see a changing definition of government responsibility, a weakening connection between accessible social opportunities and demonstrated economic performance, and a varying expression of the tenets of Social Darwinism.

Although the book refers to laws of a number of states, it focuses on those of Pennsylvania. The laws of the Commonwealth appear particularly useful, for from its earliest decades Pennsylvania has contained a culturally diverse population that has dealt with problems of both rural and urban areas and thus can offer a broad and varied group of problems for consideration. By demonstrating the institutionalization of prevailing values, Pennsylvania's legislation shows that attitudes about physical impairment both shape and are shaped by the collective actions of American society.

The inquiry into national legislation covers the period from the 1770s to the 1920s. Because much evidence indicates that the events and social thought preceding the Vocational Rehabilitation Act of 1920 shaped the "disability legislation," and the social responses to it, of subsequent decades,[30] special attention is paid to the early twentieth century. Brief references to legislation of the later 1900s (and the first Supreme Court test of section 504 of the Vocational Rehabilitation Act of 1973) appear throughout the book in order to demonstrate the persistence of disabling language and assumptions.

To develop the thesis that legislation promotes disability by conditioning the social status of physically handicapped people, the book advances five major arguments.

1. A substantial part of the devaluation, and therefore the disablement, of handicapped people can be traced to the American conceptions of individualism and responsibility. These conceptions became justifications for treating handicapped people in what appeared to be a cost effective manner.

Much of the social treatment of handicapped people depends on the general society's perceptions of their potential for economic usefulness. The relationship between the general public and handicapped people appears to be governed by a concern for cost effectiveness—a concern that will be variously described as a consequence of political individualism, an ethic of efficiency, and a doctrine of human capital. An analysis of early legislation shows that in one form or another, the emphasis on cost effectiveness led to the exclusion and segregation of handicapped people. Later laws and public documents indicate that the same principle of economics was the officially asserted justification of their rehabilitation and education. However, just as the dictates of a law may not measure actual societal behavior, so "official assertions" may be only poor representations of real motives.

Many explanations of society's devaluation of physically abnormal people are based on the religious connections between physical defect and moral defect, and on the beliefs that such theological precepts are proper guides to economic practice. The corollary that holds handicapped individuals responsible for their own physical defect seems especially clear in America's tendency to justify devaluation with the concepts of Social Darwinism. The disablement associated with religious principles probably can be attributed to a broad range of determinants. At one extreme one can identify politically forceful fundamentalist religious connections between biological wholeness and virtue (and the converse). At the other extreme are disabling practices based on the theological tenets that demand concern for the welfare of other people. But despite the many disabling effects of religion, it also seems likely that some aspect of the treatment of the handicapped population expresses the political ethic of individualism. Perhaps the certainty with which either extreme of these religious precepts is held obscures the idea of a possible secular determinant.

While imputations of personal responsibility for a physical impairment clearly exist, one can also point to another level of responsibility—expectations that each individual is responsible not for his or her own condition but for coping with its consequences. For example, from one point of view, the federal rehabilitation laws embody a congressional idea that while disability may be a national problem, it is at the same time a personal problem to be dealt with by personal means. Laws that mandate physical accessibility seem to express a third kind of responsibility: they permit handicapped people the ability to choose the degree and kind of social participation they desire.[31]

2. By directly or obliquely influencing legislation, the philosophies and practices of nineteenth-century philanthropy reinforced negative beliefs about handicapped people. In turn these beliefs informed later government action.

Although the theory of Social Darwinism was not formally articulated until the late nineteenth century, the problem of defining the "truly needy" has been a source of political tension throughout American history. A major expression of this tension—the nation's traditional reluctance to allocate public resources to the ablebodied poor—is described in Michael Katz's analysis of America's social welfare policies.[32] In order to justify public giving, therefore, it is likely that society had to label *any* beneficiary as "impotent." As a consequence, both physical disorder and dependence on the public treasury appear to have been determining factors in the attributed helplessness of physically handicapped people.

Another connection between charity and disability is suggested by Talcott Parsons' theory that society places persons whom it calls "sick" in an identifiable social role.[33] According to his thesis, occupants of the "sick role" are expected to pay for public largesse either by recovering (and then beginning or resuming a contributing role) or by dying—an alternative engendering in society the gratification of having given without material return. Thus the many handicapped people whose physical disorder is permanent remain in a position of indebtedness—a position that probably accounts for at least some portion of their socially conferred devaluation.

In theoretical papers that discuss social welfare policy, Kenneth Boulding[34] and Robert Pruger[35] point to a similar problem. Indeed, these writers clarify this source of disability when they propose that any persons who use public resources without perceived repayment to society will be publicly devaluated. This basis for allocating public resources points to the idea of equity (fairness) that underlies much human behavior, and in turn suggests the usefulness of identifying the parameters of equity in the treatment of physically handicapped people.

A mechanism proposed by Thomas Szasz suggests that even erroneous assignment to the sick role of people with long-term or permanent physical disorders does not diminish their consequent devaluation. In *The Myth of Mental Illness*,[36] Szasz looks at consequences of applying the sick label to persons who suffer not from an illness but from what he calls "problems in living"—diminished or distorted abilities to behave appropriately. (According to Szasz, only deviation from the organic standard of the anatomically and physiologically normal brain may properly be labeled psychological illness.) He asserts that those whom society authorizes to apply the label of illness hold inordinate power over people's lives, for such labeling not only relieves "ill" persons of responsibility for their actions, but relieves society of the necessity to fully value them. Perhaps the mechanism basic to this element of devaluation can be identified by thinking about Robert Merton's "Self-Fulfilling Prophecy."[37]

3. The medical/pathological paradigm of "disability legislation" effected a shift from physical inferiority to social inferiority by forcing an emphasis on the handicapped individual, and by discouraging acknowledgment of socially created sources of deviance.

Evidence in this book indicates that physically abnormal persons are permitted to enter the social mainstream *on the terms* of the ablebodied majority. Furthermore, efforts that focus on adjusting persons to fit into existing social structures do not appear to foster a political condition that makes social participation a matter of individual choice. Part of this failure may derive from the paradigm basic to "disability legislation."

In traditional medical views, the long-term or permanent functional limitations produced by physical impairments are called disability. Recent medical textbooks go further, and construe disability as a variable dependent upon characteristics of motivation and adaptability as well as upon the limiting residue of disease or injury. However, both sets of medical views consider *personal* dysfunction a sufficient criterion for disability. These orthodox views seem appropriate to medical concerns of diagnosis and treatment of the physically impaired individual. But in many instances the same medical conceptions shape public policy as well.

The concept that the assessment of physical abnormality varies with social roles to be performed is central to this book. (Wolfensberger's recent work[38] articulates this concept by referring to "normalization" as "social role valorization.") However, to regard disability as a transactional product of handicapped people and their social environments, an ecological paradigm, not a medical model, should guide public policy. By its definition, an ecological paradigm would prompt inquiry into the interactions between people's functional limitations and their environments. Its operation would probably encourage lawmakers to direct remedial strategies to the structures of the general society as well as to the persons of physically impaired people.

Although workmen's compensation laws and "Special Education" programs provide what is probably the clearest view of the medical paradigm, social treatment of wounded soldiers also discloses the medical basis of "disability legislation." Since the Revolutionary War, pensions for veterans of American wars have been given upon proof of war-induced limitations in bodily function. To be sure, techniques of assessment have become increasingly sophisticated. Nevertheless, such pensions continue to be formulated according to measures of intra-individual physical capacities. They generally are not structured to take account of the veteran's educational and economic status or of his or her "non-veteran" roles. This paradigm continues to guide the definitions of disability in twentieth century laws, for despite their anti-discriminatory basis, contemporary legislative responses often fail to assure the integration of many handicapped people.

4. The several forms of segregation characteristic of American education classify individuals with physical handicaps as "the handicapped." By forcing individuals into a category defined by physical defect, the stereotypy associated with this traditional segregation has worked

through the institutions of education to help build an equation between physical handicap and social handicap.

Until the twentieth century, one or another form of segregation characterized the various laws that dealt with handicapped people. For example, laws of the Province of Pennsylvania either expelled handicapped people or forbade their immigration. Although the demands of nineteenth century legislation never approached this extreme of exclusion, physically abnormal recipients of government support were kept separate from those with able bodies. An 1896 U.S. Supreme Court decision that dealt with racial equality may help to explain this practice. Though the finding in that case, *Plessy v. Ferguson*,[39] did not mandate segregation, it has frequently been argued that by permitting that condition, *Plessy* contributed to attributions of inferiority to American blacks. An effect similar to this has probably emerged from government tolerance of the segregation of people with physical handicaps. Furthermore, the implication in *Plessy* that social equality can exist without political equality, may partially explain the practices of charities and educational systems that continue to keep handicapped citizens apart from the majority population.

The several forms of segregation promoted by American education also help to account for the stereotypical responses that generate devaluation.[40] In the early years of the United States, segregation probably represented what was thought to be the proper atmosphere for teaching children with physical defects.[41] Such children were educated either in association with hospitals or in institutions founded and maintained by private philanthropic efforts. Techniques of teaching blind, deaf, and mentally retarded youngsters were often copies of those developed by European physicians and educators.[42] When American states initiated care, they continued the segregated structure characteristic of the private enterprises. For example, reports of Pennsylvania's Commission on Charities of the 1870s reveal that physically defective children—no matter their specific impairment—were educated apart from ablebodied children.

In some instances, specialized schools were established to teach the particular skills (for example, lip reading, sign language, Braille, and mobility training) that some children would need to function in society. To the extent that Pennsylvania's case is representative, however, the segregation built into public or publicly supported educational institutions *did not depend on the need to learn particular skills*. Integration of handicapped children in schools was apparently thought to be unnecessary, to be beyond the propriety of governmental concern, to be impossible to bring about by any political action—or perhaps it was not thought about at all.

This book points out a number of factors that contribute to the American habit of segregation. For example, we will see that the desire to punish moral inferiority may motivate the practice of forced segregation. Segregation may also represent an efficient method for dealing with children unable to adhere to standards of material productivity. In addition, Ann Shearer proposes that the participation of mentally retarded people in decisions concerning their living arrangements[43] threatens the usual assumption that handicapped people should be grateful for their care. This idea may also help to explain the absence of integration. However rationalized, though, segregation almost surely generates segregation. Children educated apart from ablebodied cohorts may fail to learn the social and interpersonal skills necessary to comfortable interaction with ablebodied adults. (Ablebodied persons, likewise, are denied opportunities for learning to interact with handicapped people.) Members of the general population may thus decide that imposing segregation represents a benevolent compliance with the desires of the handicapped population.[44]

When it eventually became clear that handicapped children would become handicapped adults, apparently no thought was given to accommodating society to the child. Educational efforts remained rooted in expectations that the child should be changed to fit into the general society. In the twentieth century the same expectation seems to characterize Special Education. The mandated emphasis on diagnosis and formulation of individualized programs clearly is helpful to many children with special educational needs. The resulting separateness often is not helpful, though, for it appears to attribute difference to the children rather than to the needs that they present. The presence of two groups of teachers instead of a single group trained to teach all children seems to reflect the belief that two different groups of children exist. Indeed, parallel systems of education, instead of a single system created to deal with all children, appear to acknowledge that physical status is a legitimate differentiating criterion. There may be no way to be fair either to "gifted" students or to "learning disabled" students other than to assign children to classrooms according to their willingness and ability to learn. But to make classroom assignments on the basis of the physical condition of the child is fair to no one.

Beliefs that legislated integration will prevent or abolish negative beliefs about physical abnormality seem to ignore the categorization implicit in the idea of special education. Although the doctrine of non-discrimination has become the legal basis of society's treatment of physically handicapped people, their thoroughly institutionalized devaluation contributes to a continuing civil inferiority.

5. One element of the disability of handicapped people can be traced to the nation's emphasis on vocational education.

According to records of congressional hearings in 1914,[45] European (especially German) systems of public education aroused fears that the ninety-three percent "drop-out" rate in American public schools would result in a citizenry unfit to wage the trade wars to come. The commission that President Wilson appointed to examine this situation recommended an extensive program of vocational education as a solution. After months of congressional committee hearings with favorable testimony from representatives of labor organizations, manufacturers and members of the teaching profession, a bill that called for states to develop vocational programs for public school students was introduced. If these locally initiated programs were approved by a Federal Board of Vocational Education, they were to be partially financed by the federal government.

The presence of this structure, conditioned by the traditional view of education as a means of promoting self-support, appears in large part to account for schemes that channel handicapped children into vocational education. Their disproportionate placement in programs of vocational education constitutes another form of segregation, and their consequent overrepresentation in manual trades appears to contribute to society's stereotypic ideas about their competence.

Since the specific purpose of this study is to relate disability to legislative responses of the American majority, two issues important to the process of the social construction of disability lie beyond its boundaries. The first is the accessibility of medical care. There can be little doubt that individual and cultural variations in both the provision and acceptance of medical therapy bear on disability as a social creation. The second has to do with the different meanings that subgroups attach to physical abnormality. The research on American children conducted by Richardson[46] and by Goodman[47] indicates such variation. These researchers concluded that preferential rankings of drawings of children with physical abnormalities are determined by values associated with the gender and the ethnic background of the subjects. The studies are unusual, for although there are many anecdotal descriptions of prejudice and many speculative analyses of its sources, there are relatively few systematic attempts at its explanation. Because the problems of ethnic and gender variations in the process of constructing disability are so important to the formulation of policy, the issues raised by this research need further study.

Notes

1. The idea of social construction is the basis of Peter L. Berger and Thomas Luckmann's *The Social Construction of Reality.*
2. Barrington Moore, *Reflections on the Causes of Human Misery and upon Certain Proposals to Eliminate Them,* p. 10.
3. Howard S. Becker, ed., *Outsiders: Studies in the Sociology of Deviance,* p. 9.
4. E.g., Edwin M. Schur, *Labeling Deviant Behavior: Its Sociological Implications; Interpreting Deviance;* Walter R. Gove, ed., *The Labeling of Deviance.*
5. Robert Bogdan and Steven J. Taylor, *Inside Out: The Social Meaning of Mental Retardation,* p. 7.
6. Robert A. Scott, *The Making of Blind Men: A Study of Adult Socialization,* p. 14.
7. Seymour B. Sarason and John Doris, *Psychological Problems in Mental Deficiency,* p. 34.
8. Gordon W. Allport, *The Nature of Prejudice.*
9. E.g., Erving Goffman, *Stigma: Notes on the Management of Spoiled Identity;* Irwin Katz, *Stigma: A Social Psychological Analysis.* Both Goffman and Katz make the point that the term "stigma" refers not simply to the attributes of discredited people, but to the syndrome of ambiguous, uncertain, responses to them. Katz's work also presents a number of experiments aimed at clarifying the situational correlates of particular responses.
10. Eliot Friedson, "Disability as Social Deviance," p. 72. Similar definitions are basic to Goffman's classic work, *Stigma,* to many of the essays edited by Howard Becker in *The Other Side: Perspectives on Deviance,* and to the thoughtful writing that characterizes Beatrice A. Wright's *Physical Disability—A Psychosocial Approach.*
11. Gerald Gordon et al., *Disease, the Individual and Society,* pp. 44–45.
12. C. Wright Mills, *The Sociological Imagination,* esp. pp. 8–10.
13. Robert K. Merton's work, esp. "Social Structure and Anomie."
14. E.g., Gary Athelstan, ed., *The Disabled Worker: Overcoming the System's Barriers.* Nancy C. Kutner and Donna R. Brogan's "Disability Labeling vs. Rehabilitation Rhetoric for the Chronically Ill: A Case Study in Policy Contradictions" demonstrates the disabling effect caused by the easy access of some patients with end-stage renal disorder to federal disability income benefits.
15. E.g., F. M. Baker, R. J. Baker, and R. S. McDaniel, "Denormalizing Practices in Rehabilitation Facilities;" W. A. Crunk, Jr., "A Study of Attitudes Toward the Severely Disabled Among Five Rehabilitation Groups;" David J. Vail, *Dehumanization and the Institutional Career.*
16. Wolf Wolfensberger, "The Origin and Nature of Our Institutional Models;" *The Principle of Normalization in Human Services.*
17. Wolf Wolfensberger, *Normalization,* p. 96.
18. Ibid., p. 28.
19. Ibid., p. 34.
20. E.g., Susan Sontag, *Illness as Metaphor;* L. Kriegel, "Uncle Tom and Tiny Tim: Some Reflections on the Cripple as Negro;" Leslie Fiedler, *Freaks: Myths and Images of the Secret Self;* W. Gellman, "Roots of Prejudice Against the Handicapped."

21. E.g., C. J. VanderKolk, "Physiological Measures as a Means of Assessing Reactions to the Disabled;" Robert Kleck, "Physical Stigma and Nonverbal Cues Emitted in Face-to-Face Interaction;" Tamara Dembo, Gloria Ladieu Leviton, and Beatrice A. Wright, "Adjustment to Misfortune: A Problem of Social Psychological Rehabilitation;" Gloria Ladieu, Dan L. Adler, and Tamara Dembo, "Studies in Adjustment to Visible Injuries: Social Acceptance of the Injured."

22. E.g., J. R. and L. M. Hanks, "The Physically Handicapped in Certain Non-Occidental Societies;" E. and M. Chigier, "Attitudes to Disability of Children in the Multi-Cultural Society of Israel;" M. Jaques et al., "Cultural Attitudes Toward Disability: Denmark, Greece and the United States."

23. E.g., Carl E. Obermann, *A History of Vocational Rehabilitation in America;* E. D. Berkowitz, *Rehabilitation: The Federal Government's Response to Disability, 1935–1954.*

24. Monroe Berkowitz, William G. Johnson, and Edward H. Murphy, *Public Policy Toward Disability.*

25. E.g., Santa Clara Law Review, "History of Unequal Treatment: The Qualifications of Handicapped Persons as a 'Suspect Class' under the Equal Protection Clause."

26. E.g., S. A. Levitan and R. Taggart, *Jobs for the Disabled.*

27. E.g., Irving Kenneth Zola, *Missing Pieces: A Chronicle of Living With A Disability.*

28. E.g., John Gliedman and William Roth for the Carnegie Council on Children, *The Unexpected Minority: Handicapped Children in America;* the participant observation study by A. and S. Dibner, *Integration or Segregation for the Physically Handicapped Child?.* See also the large number of articles centering on contemporary education: e.g., A. Abeson and J. Zettel, "The End of the Quiet Revolution: The Education for All Handicapped Children Act of 1975;" Evelyn Deno, "Special Education as Developmental Capital."

29. Thos. T. H. Wan, "Correlates and Consequences of Severe Disabilities."

30. Oliver C. Schroeder, Jr.'s article, "The Law Speaks: Disability and Legal Practice," says, however, that because the Rehabilitation Act of 1973 is based on the concept of anti-discrimination, it differs analytically from the Act of 1920.

31. Such laws were not enacted until physically handicapped people, rather than only their advocates, pressed for them. Their demands were rationalized by constitutionally-guaranteed rights to political equality, and their organized protests were clearly modeled after many of the strategies of the civil rights movement.

32. Michael B. Katz, *In the Shadow of the Poorhouse: A Social History of Welfare in America.*

33. Talcott Parsons, "Deviant Behavior and the Mechanisms of Social Control," *The Social System,* pp. 249–325.

34. Kenneth Boulding, "The Boundaries of Social Policy."

35. Robert Pruger, "Social Policy: Unilateral Transfer or Reciprocal Exchange."

36. Thomas S. Szasz, *The Myth of Mental Illness.*

37. Robert K. Merton, "The Self-Fulfilling Prophecy."

38. Wolf Wolfensberger, "Social Role Valorization: A Proposed New Term for the Principle of Normalization;" "Social Role Valorization: A New Insight, and a New Term for Normalization."

39. *Plessy v. Ferguson,* 163 U.S. 537 (1896).

40. In *The Making of Blind Men,* p. 32, Robert Scott argues *against* the major role of stereotypy: "Even though many of the problems that characterize encounters between sighted and blind men arise from the mechanics of interpersonal contact, it does not always follow that blind men explain these problems to themselves in this way. On the contrary, many of them apparently assume that a normal

person's behavior is caused by his beliefs. Thus, when a sighted man behaves assertively to a blind man so as to eliminate uncertainty, the blind man infers that the other's actions are caused by a belief that blindness makes him helpless. It is for this reason, I think, that blind people have placed so much stock in the notion of an elaborate, rigid stereotype of the blind."

41. Eduard Seguin's 1866 publication, *Idiocy: Its Treatment by the Physiological Method,* tells of schools for mentally retarded, blind, and deaf children that were initiated by a few American states in the mid-1800s.

42. Merle Frampton and Hugh Grant Rowell, *Education of the Handicapped,* Vol. I: *History;* Vol. II: *Problems.* For education of blind children see Vol. I, pp. 29–35, of deaf children, Vol. I, pp. 66–86, of feeble-minded children, Vol. I, pp. 179–82.

43. Ann Shearer, "The Handicapped Person," pp. 350–51.

44. The difficult problem of public transportation seems to support this sequence. Federal decisions making public intracity buses accessible to persons in wheel chairs were not accompanied by decisions to make routes to and from bus stops free of barriers. ("The Urban Mass Transportation Act of 1964, as amended, 1974"). Rather than acknowledge this cause for the infrequent use of these buses, many local agencies arrange for what they assume to be desired private (segregated) transportation.

45. U.S. Congressional Commission on National Aid to Vocational Education. *Hearings.* (63-2).

46. Stephen A. Richardson et al., "Cultural Uniformity in Reaction to Physical Disabilities."

47. Norman Goodman et al., "Variant Reactions to Physical Disabilities."

need of relief") goes beyond the idea that abilities depend on the individual's physical status and his role in society and indicates that abilities vary also with other (unnamed) social factors.

So while the early statutes of the New England colonies apparently conceived of disability as injury, and those of Virginia conceived of disability as an injury so severe as to prevent earning a livelihood, this law of the Continental Congress explicitly connected disability to social role (soldier or civilian) and implied its connection to other attributes of injured people. As indicated below, however, the belief that disability varies with the roles and characteristics of physically impaired individuals seems to have lasted only as long as the need for Revolutionary War soldiers.

If loss of a limb, or wounds rendering the soldier "incapable afterwards of getting a livelihood"[13] could be confirmed by an officer in the soldier's regiment, the injured man was to become eligible for half of his monthly pay either during his lifetime or for the duration of his disability. No specific account of why "half pay" was decided on exists in either the collection of letters and legislative proceedings that comprise the *American Archives*[14] of 1774, 1775, and 1776, or the *Secret Journals of the Congress of the Confederation.*[15] The well-known arguments of some states against contributing funds to a central government, however, indicate that half pay might well have been a congressional compromise between gratitude to the soldier and respect for the treasury.

In 1778, General Washington asked Congress to promise *all* officers half pay for their lifetimes.[16] But financial constraints apparently drove Congress to resolve instead that all military officers should "after the conclusion of the war, be entitled to receive annually, *for the term of seven years,* if they live so long, one half of the present pay. . . ." [my emphasis].[17] In 1780, however, General Washington expressed grave concern that the grant's inadequacy contributed to poor army morale and Congress then agreed to provide half pay for life.[18]

Washington's focus on the well-being of officers may of course have been guided by a personal vision of a proper social order as well as by concern for an efficient army. His recommendations do not indicate that his actions were motivated by a personal devaluation of physically impaired people; they seem informed only by social and military criteria.

This discussion of early military pension arrangements is hardly meant to deny, though, that the often discussed factors of fear and superstition and prejudice are major sources of the devaluation of handicapped people. The point is that these sources may not always or completely explain this devaluation. As is the case with the uneven application of the doctrine of human capital, some element of disability is rooted in legislative responses that have no direct relation to feelings about handicapped people. (Clearly, economic and political concerns may justify such feelings.)

The next chapter will discuss workmen's compensation legislation *vis-à-vis* disability. But it seems appropriate now to point out the possible effect of this Revolutionary War law on the structure of those later statutes. The eighteenth-century decisions that recipients of public aid should receive a portion of their previous salary may have expressed the idea that *any* disbursements of public money should represent a fraction of previous private earnings. Because workmen's compensation laws were developed at a time when fundamentalist Protestantism was a considerable political force in the nation, most writers have attributed the direct relationship between benefits and the worker's previous wage to the practice of linking personal worth to work. However, these eighteenth-century military pension laws suggest that this usual explanation is not entirely satisfactory. The structure of compensation laws may reflect social class distinctions as legitimate criteria for allocating public funds. They may have little to do with the Protestant correlation of work and value. A parallel argument applies to Blanche D. Coll's discussion of the principle of "less eligibility" ("assistance must be less than the lowest going wage").[19] Coll attributes this system of allocating public resources to prevailing notions about the moral character of paupers. Although the case for relating "less eligibility" to moral considerations is compelling, it is also possible that the doctrine exemplifies a habitual method of dealing with public resources.

Though compensation legislation may not reflect a general social devaluation of physically abnormal people, there are many indications that it did promote devaluation and disability. Much of the material in the next chapter specifies these consequences of the laws.

The 1776 Resolution further directed that each man disabled to the extent that he could no longer serve in the army or the navy, but who was "not totally disabled from getting a livelihood":

> shall receive such monthly sum toward his subsistence as shall
> be judged adequate by the assembly or other representative body
> of the state where he belongs or resides, upon application to
> them for that purpose, provided the same doth not exceed his
> half pay.[20]

Permitting states to grant pensions in proportion to a degree of disability assessed by their own officials may have been an attempt to pander to their sense of sovereignty. Moreover, the many delegates who resisted the idea of a centralized government probably also resisted caring for soldiers whose service affirmed the existence of a nation. At any rate, Congress was forced to repeat its recommendations several times.[21] The 1785 law that urged states to adopt plans for dealing with injured soldiers ended with the assurance "[T]hat each State shall have credit in the payment of its annual quota to the United States for such sum or sums as may be advanced to invalids according to the foregoing regulations."[22] Enacting this promise points out, as clearly as the speeches of any intransigent state delegate, the fragile legitimacy of the national government.

By asserting that disability does not necessarily excuse one from working at an array of jobs in the army or navy, a later section of the 1776 legislation confirmed the implication in the preface that disability does not mean uselessness:

> Provided, that all such officers and soldiers that may be entitled to the aforesaid pension, and are found to be capable of doing guard or garrison duty, shall be formed in a corps of invalids, and subject to the said duty; and all officers, marines, and seamen of the navy who shall be entitled to the pension aforesaid, and shall be found capable of doing any duty on board the navy, or any department thereof, shall be liable to be so employed:[23]

This portion of the Resolution was elaborated in a statute (quoted at length below) enacted the following year. Its theme seems to anticipate the philosophy held by many of the citizen-organizations of the 1970s and 1980s. These politically active groups insist that proper government policy should maintain expectations of physically abnormal individuals that differ in degree, not in quality, from those held of ablebodied people.

> *Resolved,* That a Corps of Invalids be formed consisting of eight Companies. . . . This Corps to be employed, in Garrisons and for Guards, in Cities and other Places, where Magazines or Arsenals are placed; as also to serve as Military School for Young Gentlemen, previous to their being appointed to marching Regiments, for which purpose, all the Subaltern Officers, when off duty, shall be obliged to attend a Mathematical School, appointed for the purpose to learn Geometry, Arithmetick, vulgar and decimal Fractions and the extractions of Roots. And that the Officers of this Corps, shall be obliged to contribute, one day's pay in every Month, and Stoppages shall be made of it accordingly, for the purpose of purchasing a Regimental Library of the most approved Authors on Tacticks and the Petite Guere.

> That some Officers from this Corps be constantly employed in
> the Recruiting Service, in the Neighbourhood of the places, they
> shall be stationed in, that all Recruits so made, shall be brought
> into the Corps and drilled and afterwards draughted into other
> Regiments as occasion shall require.[24]

The statute also implies that one's physical status did not diminish the
expectations inherent in the concept of *noblesse oblige*. Perhaps by illus-
trating the primacy of social class distinctions, this traditional practice
provides another indication that in 1776 one's physical handicap neither
reflected nor conferred devaluation by the general society. The Corps was
formalized in June, 1777,[25] when Congress elected a colonel to be its head,
and shortly thereafter[26] appointed its paymaster.

After its deliberations of July 16, 1777, Congress issued newspaper
advertisements notifying injured soldiers who had already been discharged
of the opportunity to be evaluated for joining—at full pay—the Corps of
Invalids. The notice ended by appealing to soldiers' desires to display to
new recruits their status as veterans of especially good repute:

> As this corps is intended, not only as a provision for disabled
> officers and soldiers, but as a school for propagating military
> knowledge and discipline, no officers apply but such as produce
> ample certificates of their having served with reputation, and
> having supported good characters, both as citizens and as
> soldiers.[27]

The 1778 provision that any qualified disabled soldier who refused to join
the Corps of Invalids should be "struck off the list of pensioners"[28] unless
he was so "peculiarly circumstanced"[29] that the executives of his state
believed he should be excepted, may have represented another attempt to
indulge the states while guarding the treasury.

In 1778, Congress extended the scope of military pensions by establishing annual payments for the widow of any officer killed in military
service equal in amount to half of his pay. No pensions were given the
widows of private soldiers.[30] Beginning in 1836,[31] however, legislation
granted pensions to the widows of any soldiers killed in the military;
similar laws remain in force.

Almost as soon as the United States of America was established, the
country assumed the duty of paying the pensions of Revolutionary War
soldiers.[32] Although an act of 1792 that provided for a uniform militia
throughout the nation[33] again mandated public care of wounded soldiers,
there were no longer any arrangements for a Corps of Invalids.

Shortly thereafter, legislation provided that a list of pensioners be published "in one or more . . . newspapers . . . adding to such publication, the time when the act regulating the claims to invalid pensions expires."[34] While publication surely was a means of accounting for public money, it also highlighted the dependency of particular individuals on public funds. Perhaps it is the case that having become independent of the contribution of each citizen, the nation could boast about the existence of dependent citizens. If so, the motivation of a law by national pride is another example that factors unrelated to attitudes about physical infirmity contribute to constructing disability.

These resolutions permit several inferences:

1. The nation decided that injured military men should be helped by public resources. However, the argument that the *form* of the public's care of disabled soldiers often reflects a concern with usefulness does not suggest that the *fact* of public involvement derives from other than a feeling of gratitude. For while the forms and the degrees of public involvement have varied, the belief that wounded soldiers should be objects of public care has remained constant throughout the nation's history.

2. Perceptions of public need (to a large extent in the form of military need) helped to shape the laws about disability. Virginia's colonial legislation indicates that the idea of disability changed from an unqualified label for serious injury to a concept that varied with social roles and with socioeconomic status.

3. Attitudes about physical impotence only partially account for the legislation that has dealt with the handicapped population, for ideas about the proper use of public money and the proper behavior of social classes have had an impact on such laws. Furthermore, the fact that wounded soldiers had little or no influence on the structure of their pensions suggests that predominantly negative ideas about any beneficiaries of public care were also operative.

4. America's understanding of disability seems to have affected the concept of national obligation. When physically abnormal people were considered to be useful to the nation, legislation mandated that they act as citizens. When they were considered to be useless, the sense of civil obligation basic to these laws apparently gave way to ideas that society's responsibility was fulfilled by the kindly provision of pensions or alms houses.[35]

5. Decisions about how to deal with wounded soldiers exemplify the struggle for a satisfactory balance between the obligations of individual states and those of the national government.

Although there are no certain causal links between early policies and those of today, the substance and format of these early laws probably laid the groundwork for contemporary legislative and administrative policy. While this proposed process points to a general mechanism of legislative habit, it also shows that laws, as both causes and effects, are central to the construction of disability.

Early Twentieth-Century Legislation

Public Vocational Education

In 1914, the Congress created a Commission on National Aid to Vocational Education.[36] The Commission's hearings and mail surveys testified to the existence of three problems: many students left high school because courses did not teach them to earn a livelihood; young adults were unprepared to work in the nation's factories and farms; the low productivity of an unskilled work force affected the nation's ability to compete in the market place.[37] Responding to the threat to the public welfare inherent in these problems, the Commission declared vocational education to be a national obligation and set forth the criteria for federal activity with this paragraph:

> The Federal Government is acting in cooperation with the States in doing many things which otherwise would remain undone or be but slowly and imperfectly done. The Government carries on many enterprises permitted by the Constitution and necessary to the general welfare which are interstate in interest and character and which could not be conducted satisfactorily by the separate States.[38]

After inquiring into systems of vocational education in Canada and in several European countries, the Commission recommended that the national government aid the states in developing educational programs in agriculture, trade, commerce and home economics. Federal grants were to be used for training and paying teachers, and were to be allocated in proportion to state populations. Unlike previous national involvement in education,[39] though, this was not to be unrestricted aid. Grants were to be given states only if a Federal Board approved their plans for vocational education.

The Commission justified its scheme of federal/state cooperation by linking the issue of state obligation to the problem of financial constraints:

A State can not be expected to devote large sums from her public revenues to the making of good workmen for the benefit of other States. Only out of a common fund like the National Treasury can the burden be equalized and adjusted so that each State may in justice be expected to meet the obligation resting upon its schools.[40]

By 1916, committees of the House and Senate had transformed the Commission's recommendations into a bill for congressional consideration.[41] Much of the subsequent debate centered on questions of how to allocate federal aid and how to construct and organize the proposed Federal Board. However, some of the congressional speeches expressed concern with other issues. Examination of the record reveals, for example, that most supporters emphasized that the bill was needed to wage the economic battle expected to follow the European War. Furthermore, to arguments that every available dollar should be used to arm the nation, adherents replied with statements like Senator Page's: "If something is not done to improve our citizenship our political fabric will be shaken to its foundations . . . an educated and prosperous citizenship is our only safety."[42] In similar fashion, warnings of an unnecessary federal bureaucracy were met by persuasive declarations of need for a system of gathering and communicating vocational information to the states.

Many supporters of the bill argued for the sheer virtue of work—and thus of vocational education. For example, pleas for individualism and for the principle of minimal federal intervention were overcome by assertions that because America is a working nation, legislation to "make the most out of brain, heart and hand"[43] represented a desirable and proper function of the federal government. This spiritual dimension was stretched even further when the bill was extolled as an expression of the nation's values of the dignity of work and the disgrace of idleness.[44]

A variety of other principles were touched upon by proponents and critics of the bill. For example, Representative Finis Garrett phrased the "state-autonomy" argument in the terms of proper legislative procedure:

It is proposed, just as was in the roads bill, to coerce the State through the most powerful instrumentality of coercion that now exists in this country, and that is through the use of the taxing power.

I do not believe . . . that that principle ought to apply in legislation.[45]

Several congressmen envisioned vocational education as a mechanism that would promote democracy by strengthening the middle class.[46] Presumably as a consequence, much debate revolved about the study of home economics. Indeed, one of the most persuasive arguments for its inclusion in the bill held that teaching home economics would lower the divorce rate and would decrease childhood mortality.[47]

One senator saw the bill not only as an example of fairness that would elicit the respect and loyalty of immigrants, but as a means to solve many of the nation's social problems:

> The congestion of our cities is unhealthy, unprofitable, criminal producing, and, let me repeat, we must relieve that congestion by keeping our boys and girls upon the farm, and we cannot keep them there unless we so educate them that farm life is both profitable and pleasant—pleasant largely because it is profitable.[48]

But the worries about state sovereignty and federal interference indicate that the central theoretical question of the debates was the likely effect of conditional grants on America's traditional structure of federalism. The House Committee on Education and the Senate Committee on Education and Labor concluded that grants to states contingent on federal approval of their plans would effect better programs of vocational education than would outright grants. Nevertheless, many lawmakers saw such awards as little more than bribes that would diminish the sovereignty of states and distort, if not destroy, the traditional American system of federalism. For example,

> The contribution to the States is contemptible in amount, in derogation of the dignity of the States, and hurtful to the system of public schools within the States, in that it will teach the taxpayers more and more to rely on Federal appropriations, but it suffices to tempt gentlemen from the traditions and principles of their party, the party of Thomas Jefferson.[49]

However, perhaps because the substance of debate was education, the fears may not have been entirely those of a threat to the traditional structure of federalist government. The hidden subject might have been the preservation of parents' control of their children. This point is suggested by a sequence of events that occurred several decades earlier. In 1862, despite bitter protests of unconstitutionality, the Congress assigned portions of federal land for the establishment of state colleges. But because the repeated proposals for federal aid to common schools that were made in the 1870s and 1880s failed to become law, the education of *young* children appears to represent other passions. The considerable anecdotal material that indicates that ablebodied people often treat handicapped adults as children may partially explain both the nineteenth-century denial of federal aid and the failure of the United States to assure education to all handicapped children before 1975.[50]

The variety of theoretical elements in the debates that preceded the bill's 1917 enactment[51] permits several kinds of analyses. One might look at the bill, for example, as a theological demand for useful work or as a capitalist demand for productive work. Furthermore, one might see the bill as a reflection of the beliefs of Social Darwinism, as a source of the disproportionately small number of women in rehabilitation programs, as a crude effort to stimulate partisan loyalty, or as a means for maintaining the order of the social classes.

Vocational Rehabilitation for Soldiers

By the time of the Great War, medical procedures and their availability had improved to the extent of making survival possible for a large number of wounded soldiers. This result of technological advancement probably induced Congress to decide that the citizenry as a whole would suffer if this substantial population segment were to remain financially unproductive and a long-term drain upon public resources.

A second possible consequence of the presence of so many wounded soldiers can be inferred from a particular segment of Sarason and Doris's review of America's treatment of mentally retarded people. In this portion of their analysis, the authors explain the diminishing primacy of hereditarian theories of mental deficiency:

> When poverty was remote, its victims could well be assumed to merit no better. But when oneself and one's loved ones were impoverished it was obviously more rational to recognize that it was the system that was at fault and not the individual. Thus the [G]reat [D]epression led to an emphasis on environmental and social factors as the root of social ills, and a de-emphasis on hereditarily inferior strains of the human race.[52]

Available records do not permit comparison to 1776 of the proportion of wounded veterans to the entire population. It is likely though, that when the many wounded soldiers of the World War became visible, individual human problems became more clear to more people, and the explanatory principle offered by Sarason and Doris was operative.

Furthermore, as measured by congressional responsiveness to their perceived interests, the political strength of veterans had increased considerably. In the atmosphere of rising societal sensitivity, and in the face of rising political potency of an already favored group, the national government apparently concluded that it was obliged to do more for its injured soldiers than simply reward them with some form of maintenance. The fact that a system for the vocational education of high school students was already in place appeared to suggest to the Congress a way to deal with this problem.

The report introducing the military rehabilitation bill stated:

> Both from the standpoint of saving a multiplicity of national boards and from the standpoint of fixing this work in a board already designated by Congress to take care of vocational education—a board which has accumulated, during the past year, a fund of experience in handling problems of vocational reeducation and which has organized a staff of experts specially fitted to assume this new work—the measure has placed the control and direction of the work of vocational rehabilitation, as distinguished from functional rehabilitation, in the Federal Board for Vocational Education.[53]

Assertions that specialists in vocational education are able to deal with wounded soldiers and that vocational rehabilitation can be separated from "functional rehabilitation" are, at the very least, questionable. Incorporating these beliefs into the law almost certainly was part of the formation of disability.

In the debates concerning the bill, Congress assured itself of the virtue of federal attempts to convert wounded soldiers into useful civilians. But the predominant justification for the proposed legislation was its economic value to the nation. The records of the Congress's deliberations suggest that only that kind of federal action which enhances usefulness is proper. Nothing in the portions of the *Congressional Record* related to this bill suggests that "usefulness" had several forms; usefulness apparently was perceived only as the ability to contribute to national economic productivity.

In 1918, Congress unanimously enacted the law "[T]o provide for vocational rehabilitation and return to civil employment of disabled persons discharged from the military or naval forces of the United States. . . ."[54] But despite its mandate that

[there] shall be furnished by the said board, where vocational rehabilitation is feasible, such course of vocational rehabilitation
as the board shall prescribe and provide[,][55]

the Board of Vocational Education actually trained very few soldiers. According to the Board's monthly *Vocational Summary,*[56] by August 23,
1919—fourteen months after the passage of this statute—of the
estimated[57] 250,000 disabled servicemen, 170,405 men had contacted, or
were contacted by, the Board, 113,863 were evaluated for the likelihood
of successful vocational training, 23,388 were recommended for training,
and 7,812 were begun in a training program. As indicated below, congressional investigations considered the exclusive source of the failure indicated by these numbers to lie in the structure and implementation of this
piece of legislation.

One such group of structural problems appears to reflect the rather
naive belief that separate agencies of government would interact smoothly.
For example, in 1914 the Congress had established the Bureau of War
Risk Insurance, subsequently charging it with the assessment of disability
as well as with the financial compensation of disabled soldiers.[58] However,
the new Act required the Board of Vocational Education both to train
and to compensate soldiers whom the Bureau of War Risk had judged
compensable and whom the Board had judged "rehabilitatable." Not sur-
prisingly, the conflicting interpretations of the role of each agency resulted
in many wounded soldiers receiving no compensation. An amended law
of July 11, 1919 finally resolved these conflicts by disassociating the work
of the War Risk Bureau from that of the Board.[59]

Similar jurisdictional disputes between the Departments of War and
Navy and the Vocational Education Board were almost assured by the
Law's language:

> Whenever training is employed as a therapeutic measure by the
> War Department or the Navy Department a plan may be estab-
> lished between these agencies and the board of Vocational Edu-
> cation acting in an advisory capacity to insure, in so far as
> medical requirements permit, a proper process of training and
> the proper preparation of instructors for such training. A plan
> may also be established between the War and Navy Departments
> and the board whereby these departments shall act in an advi-
> sory capacity with the board in the care of the health of the sol-
> dier and sailor after his discharge.
>
> The board shall, in establishing its plans and rules and regula-
> tions for vocational training, cooperate with the War Depart-

ment and the Navy Department in so far as may be necessary to
effect a continuous process of vocational training.[60]

The maladministration by confused and jealous agencies and the discon-
tinuous medical care that apparently emerged from reliance on informal
"advice and cooperation" between the military and the Board were not
the only structural sources of difficulty. The Military Vocational Rehabilitation Act empowered the Board "to make such rules and regulations
as may be necessary for the proper performance of its duties. . . ."[61] Although the bulk of the 1919 *Annual Report* of the Federal Board of
Vocational Education[62] is devoted to the declaration of positive achievements, one set of figures[63] implies that the program's efficiency suffered
from disproportionate centralization: of the 22,532 men approved by the
regional districts by August 16, 1919, 10,361 still awaited a mandatory
re-evaluation by the central Board.

On September 30, 1919 a congressional resolution called for investigation of the Board.[64] When discussing the need for such an investigation,
the House Committee on Rules examined newspaper and magazine articles and received testimony from all over the country.[65] Apparently, however, this resolution was not followed by any formal investigation, and
none of the material that was gathered was ever presented to the whole
Congress.

However, another inquiry was begun in March, 1920, when Representative Simeon Fess called for the Board's investigation by the House Committee on Education.[66] This time, after hearing 2,200 pages of testimony,
this committee offered several recommendations to Congress.[67] All of the
suggestions seem based on the assumption that program inefficiency, subject to cure by reorganization and by increased funds, entirely accounted
for the poor results of the federal vocational rehabilitation program. But
both the theory that is basic to this law and the usual process of recovering
from serious wounds indicate that other reasons for the program's inef-
fectiveness may have existed.

THEORETICAL SOURCES OF FAILURE

Teaching vocations to physically intact youngsters is different from
teaching vocations—often new ones—to physically impaired adults who
have suffered physical and psychological traumas and who face the problem of readjusting to civilian life. It follows from this difference that
teachers who can instruct ablebodied children are not necessarily capable
of training physically impaired adults. One can conclude from this rea-

soning that the insufficient number of competent teachers was only in part a function of the short time and sparse funds allocated for training.

A second factor that might explain the Law's unsatisfactory result is the idea that vocational training is categorically distinct from the whole of physical rehabilitation. On the analytical level of understanding rehabilitation as a holistic effort, this distinction makes no sense. On the analytic level of identifying consequences for wounded soldiers, institutionalization of this distinction was a source of disability.

Indeed, a series of statistics from the *Vocational Summary* (1919)[68] suggests that some of the difficulty in effecting rehabilitation resulted from defining the restoration of wounded soldiers as the ability to obtain gainful employment. The numbers of soldiers registered with the Vocational Board dropped from 32,580 in March/April to 13,004 in July/August. However, the number of registrants who were actually evaluated in the same monthly periods declined from 25,649 to 8,237. It is possible that an increasing number of soldiers grew to understand that by recognizing only the vocational element in rehabilitation, the government had discredited many of their psychological and social needs. Consideration of the following evidence supports this proposition. Standard textbooks in rehabilitation medicine[69] indicate that (1) the recovery of severely injured persons often proceeds in clearly definable stages; and (2) an early period of grieving and confusion is eventually followed by one of understanding that human identity is intact. When soldiers came to realize that their physical wounds had not made their social needs different from those of ablebodied persons, and when they also came to realize that they were generally believed to be able to perform only as workers, it would seem that avoiding the government's program was a possible response.

As has been described, explanations for the program's failure published by the government (as well as by the *American Legion Weekly*[70]) invariably focused on administrative inefficiency. It seems reasonable, however, that some part of this failure had its source in this psychological reaction. Indeed, by beginning a section on therapeutic intervention with a chapter on legislation, a recent text by Vash[71] supports this explanation. The structure of Vash's book implies that part of the ability of some individuals to adjust to personal physical abnormality depends on their perceptions of the actions of society as a whole.

This same argument points out another part of the process of constructing disability. The limitation of federal action to the area of vocational rehabilitation may have taught the general population that wounded soldiers can be expected to be restored only to the work force.

ESTABLISHMENT OF BUREAU FOR VETERANS

By 1818[72] pensions were granted to any soldiers (not only those who had been injured) who had served in the Revolutionary War *and were indigent*. In that year Congress empowered the Secretary of War to deal with pension claims;[73] for, as Glasson states, "[t]he pension business had . . . become so great that Congress abandoned the attempt to participate in the[ir] detailed administration. . . ."[74]

Throughout the nineteenth century, laws providing pensions for veterans both increased the financial benefits and lessened the restrictions for them and their dependents. These trends were interrupted only occasionally. For example, in 1836[75] legislation required a widow who claimed a pension to prove that she had married before her husband had been wounded, and during and shortly after the Civil War, the federal government demanded that pensioners of earlier wars prove their loyalty to the Union.[76]

Furthermore, during most of the nineteenth century the nation awarded pensions in return for service without the condition of injury. It is interesting to note, though, that the nation did not arrange for these awards until after each war. By 1888 the National Encampment of the Grand Army of the Republic succeeded in converting its demands for promises of these so-called service pensions into a plank of the Republican party.[77] Congress, however, still made no such pledges to active soldiers, but continued to award pensions at the time of discharge. But by ultimately leading to pre-enlistment promises of service pensions, this formal recognition appears to have played a substantial role in separating society's concept of the injured veteran from that of the physically infirm civilian. With such pledges, America's treatment of soldiers has become a reward for their service to the country. While soldiers always were more highly rewarded if they were wounded, there has come to be little if any qualitative distinction between "veterans" and "handicapped veterans." The legislated (although certainly not always societal) treatment of veterans now depends only on the service they have given, not on whether they are expected to contribute again. Veterans appear to be valued for what they have done. Their value, unlike that of handicapped civilians, is no longer conditioned by their potential for economic productivity.

The Fess Report on the Board's inefficiency, and the dissatisfaction of individual soldiers and veteran organizations apparently were enough to stimulate President Harding to appoint a commission to investigate both the Board and the War Risk Bureau.[78] The Commission, headed by Charles G. Dawes, unanimously recommended that there should be one central authority for "soldier relief."[79] On April 7, 1921, the Commission issued its report, ending with a passage that articulated postwar America's feelings about its veterans:

> It cannot be too strongly emphasized that the present deplorable failure on the part of the Government to properly care for the disabled veterans is due in large part to imperfect organization of Governmental effort. There is no one in control of the whole situation. . . . No Cabinet officer or assistant secretary burdened with other duties should be the one to whom the·men charged with the welfare of the disabled saviors of our country should report. He should report directly to the President. His place should be held in the public esteem as one of the greatest honors that the President can bestow, as the service he can render should be of untold value to the nation.[80]

The persistent clamor for service pensions, the authority given the Secretary of War, and the powerful language of the Dawes report apparently all combined to prompt formation of a Veterans Bureau. The many problems of what was to become the Veterans Administration are not relevant to this book, for after this time the status of veteran rather than the status of physically handicapped person clearly governed society's treatment of injured veterans.

The legislated dependency of veterans' pensions on economic productivity has had an erratic history. One can see what is probably the last indication of this statutory relationship in the Military Rehabilitation Act of 1918. After the formation of the Veterans Bureau, the doctrine of human capital applied exclusively to handicapped civilians.

Vocational Rehabilitation for Civilians

One element of the institutionalized devaluation of people with physical impairments is reflected in society's differential treatment of handicapped soldiers and civilians. The Industrial Rehabilitation Act of 1920 shows handicapped civilians disproportionately held to standards of economic utility and more negatively labeled than wounded soldiers. This section describes the final stage in the creation of this difference.

With civilian rehabilitation legislation, American society appears to have firmly developed the notion of human capital. Despite the questionable ability of the Federal Board, but justified by this notion of relating a person's worth to his or her economic utility, legislation was introduced[81] in 1919 to extend vocational rehabilitation to "persons disabled in industry or in any legitimate occupation. . . ."[82] The bill generated intense debate about the propriety of federal help to civilians. Issues of individualism, expense, growing bureaucracy, state sovereignty, and the violation of traditional federalism—all argued in the congressional debate over vocational education for students—were re-argued. In addition several congressmen voiced concerns that the proposed legislation might overlap, or even destroy, the states' workmen's compensation laws.[83]

A few congressmen, however, saw federal care of injured workers not in economic terms but as a moral obligation consistent with the nation's traditional values. For example, Representative William Green of Iowa stated:

> I believe I have been as consistent a supporter of economy as any Member of this House. I have worked as much to keep down appropriations as any other Member. But there are some debts that this nation ought, in good conscience and honor, to pay, and one of those is the debt it owes to these men who have been crippled in building up great industries of this country.[84]

With a somewhat similar argument, Senator Joseph Walsh, a member of the Committee on Education and Labor, supported the bill by relating it to the nation's duty to promote the happiness and well-being of the family:

> I have seen repeatedly men in industrial life who have lost an arm or a leg go home to their families, and then their wife or young children forced away from home and school and obliged to support their crippled husband or father. Why should the man or woman whose only offense was that he had met with an accident in industrial life be obliged to be a dependent and bring burdens to those who naturally look to him for support? I consider it a reflection upon our foresight that we have not long ago met this industrial problem and found a solution for it. It is the Government's work to solve it.[85]

One congressman employed the model of the education of children in his discussion, and introduced into the debate what was to become the difficult issue of entitlement:

> Just as no sane man to-day opposes the idea of free education for every child, so the day will come when the same general and

universal acceptance will be given the idea that it is a governmental duty to restore and re-educate and rehabilitate every worker crippled in industry.[86]

(This passage appears to recognize the inevitability of the Education of All Handicapped Children Act.)[87]

Most of the rationale, however, was stated in terms of economics and national welfare. Representative Simeon Fess, Chairman of the House Committee on Education, exemplified this line of thought when he explained that the bill's design for salvaging human wreckage "is a cheaper and more economical plan than . . . keeping them in the poorhouse or in sanitariums."[88]

In a similar vein, Representative Clyde Kelly asserted that "this great work of human salvage means changing a national liability into a national asset."[89] Representative William Bankhead also stressed the economic value of this law:

> They say that what we offer them . . . is a proposition making appeal to the sentimentality of the members of this committee [the Whole House]. This is not essentially a sentimental bill. It is essentially an economic measure of the soundest common sense, and if you analyze it in that spirit you will see it will accomplish that result.[90]

A major aspect of disability grows out of regarding people as instruments of economic welfare. Another is rooted in the idea of "salvaging" human beings.

The bill as originally reported limited rehabilitation services to those persons who were disabled in industry.[91] But many congressmen saw the goal of national welfare as poorly served by that limit, and as logically demanding the rehabilitation of people whose physical impairments were congenital or were acquired by nonindustrial disease or injury.[92] Some congressmen agreed with federal care of certain such citizens but objected to extending the nation's resources to those whose personal life they thought distasteful. But despite the facetious attribution to the Constitution's interstate commerce clause of the eligibility of a bum whose arm is lost in a railroad accident,[93] the national welfare rationale prevailed:

> For the purpose of this Act the term "persons disabled" shall be construed to mean any person who, by reason of a physical defect or infirmity, whether congenital or acquired by accident, in-

jury, or disease, is or may be expected to be, totally or partially incapacitated for remunerative occupation[.][94]

Summary of the Early Twentieth-Century Laws

The primary justification for the 1917 act to provide vocational education was the perceived value of well-trained workers to the nation's standards of living and to its abilities to compete with other nations. Consideration of the 1918 provisions for military rehabilitation against the background of this law suggests that congressmen realized that gratitude—in the form of maintenance of injured soldiers—did not fully serve the nation's welfare. A vocational rehabilitation program that would turn soldiers into economically useful civilians apparently was seen both as an expression of gratitude and as a method to benefit the national welfare.

However, by this time veterans seemed to have become a political force powerful enough to affect the legislation that affected them. Many veterans apparently felt entitled to gratitude unmixed with concerns about national welfare—that is, to pensions not contingent upon injury. Congress appeared to agree with that feeling by creating a Veterans Bureau. When society defined veterans—injured or not—as a special class, the conception of disability, at least regarding soldiers, reverted to that held by the New England colonies. Pensions no longer distinguished between physical abnormalities and disabilities. Grants to wounded soldiers were graded on the basis of the severity of the wounds, and were unrelated to the soldier's ability to function. In addition, their dollar amount was, and continues to be, unrelated to the education or occupation or socioeconomic status of the soldier.

In contrast to this principle of reward, the Industrial Vocational Rehabilitation Act expressed an ethic of economic productivity. Its enactment resulted in substantial political and social change, for public care for physically abnormal people had traditionally been administered by the states. But when it became apparent that some of those people could be trained to work, or trained to return to work, or trained to do new work, the problem of their use was seen as a national problem, and their training became a national obligation. Subsequent chapters demonstrate the disabling quality of this human capital imperative by showing that many of the later legislative definitions of disability continue the traditional focus on gainful employment.

One purpose of this chapter has been to set forth the differences between the social treatment of medically impaired civilians and that of injured soldiers. These disparate models demonstrate the role of a theory of human capital in the construction of disability. The fact that there is no modern "Corps of Invalids" and the fact that society refuses to demand military service of physically handicapped civilians indicates that society's expectations of this population segment do not express an unambiguous rationale of human capital.

This chapter has also begun the argument that the treatment of medically impaired children to some degree serves as a model for the treatment of handicapped adults. If this modeling relationship helps to account for the uneven and uncertain application of the doctrine of human capital, inquiry into the expectations held of American children with physical defects would certainly be a useful effort.

As we have seen, consequences of the Industrial Rehabilitation Law point to issues of social and civil assimilation. Two such effects of the Law are especially pertinent to this book. For one thing, ramifications of this law's assumption that the value of physically impaired people is defined by gainful employment resulted in denying them the same opportunities of citizenship accorded the ablebodied population. Secondly, the understanding that government did nothing more to achieve their integration into society probably promoted the disabling belief that social marginality is a natural consequence of serious physical impairment.

Notes

1. Throughout this chapter the term "military" refers to armies and navies, and the term "soldiers" includes mariners. In one respect that uniformity is unwarranted, for unlike pensions for soldiers, early naval pensions depended in part on bounties seized at sea. But the generalization seems appropriate to the broad purpose of finding the conceptions of disability that laws express and the disabling consequences that they produce.

2. U.S., *An Act to provide for the promotion of vocational education. . . .* (1917).

3. U.S., *An Act to provide for vocational rehabilitation and return to civil employment of disabled persons discharged from the military . . . .* (1918).

4. U.S., *An Act to provide for the promotion of vocational rehabilitation of persons disabled in industry or otherwise . . . .* (1920).

5. M. J. Lerner, D. T. Miller and J. G. Holmes, "Deserving and the Emergence of Forms of Justice;" M. J. Lerner and C. H. Simmons, "Observer's Reaction to the Innocent Victim: Compassion or Rejection?"

6. Colony of New Plymouth, *Laws enacted in the session of 1636*, p. 106.

7. Province of the Massachusetts Bay, *An Act for Levying Souldiers, 1693,* Vol. 1, p. 135.

8. Colony of Virginia, *Act X, 1644*, Hening, Vol. 1, p. 287.

9. Colony of Virginia, *Act I, 1674 or 1675*, Hening, Vol. 2, p. 331.

10. William H. Glasson, "History of Military Pension Legislation in United States."

11. U.S. Continental Congress, *Journals of Congress,* Vol. 1, pp. 702–05, Aug. 26, 1776.

12. Ibid., p. 702.

13. Ibid.

14. Peter Force, ed., *American Archives: Consisting of A Collection of Authentick Records, State Papers, Debates and Letters and Other Notices of Publick Affairs.* Fourth Series, *From the King's Message of Mar. 7, 1774 to the Declaration of Independence by the United States in 1776.*

15. U.S., *Secret Journals of the Congress of the Confederation.*

16. U.S., *Collection of Papers Relative to Half-Pay and Commutation of Half-Pay Granted by Congress to the Officers of the Army,* pp. 3–5.

17. Ibid., p. 5.

18. Ibid., p. 9. Shortly after the grant of half pay for life, many army officers petitioned Congress for full pay "for a certain number of years" (p. 12). Cognizant that previous grants of half pay were "regarded in an unfavorable light by the citizens of some . . . states, who would prefer a compensation for a limited term of years, or by a sum in gross, to an establishment for life . . ." (p. 30), Congress resolved in 1783 that each officer "shall be entitled to receive the amount of five years full pay in money or securities, on interest at six per cent per annum, as Congress shall find most convenient, instead of the half pay promised for life . . ." (p. 31).

19. Blanche D. Coll, *Perspectives in Public Welfare: A History,* p. 15.

20. U.S. Continental Congress, *Journals of Congress,* Vol. 1, p. 703, Aug. 26, 1776.

21. Ibid., Vol. 7, p. 164, Feb. 27, 1777; Vol. 12, p. 953, Sept. 25, 1778; Vol. 26, pp. 253–254, Apr. 20, 1784; Vol. 28, pp. 51–52, Feb. 8, 1785.

22. Ibid., Vol. 28, p. 52, Feb. 8, 1785.

23. Ibid., Vol. 1, p. 705, Aug. 26, 1776.

24. Ibid., Vol. 7, pp. 288–89, Apr. 22, 1777.

25. Ibid., p. 485, June 20, 1777.

26. Ibid., Vol. 8, p. 690, Aug. 28, 1777.

27. Ibid., Vol. 7, p. 556, July 16, 1777.

28. Ibid., p. 954, Sept. 25, 1778.

29. Ibid.

30. Ibid., Vol. 34, pp. 19–20, Jan. 5, 1778.

31. U.S., *An Act granting half pay to widows or orphans whose husbands and fathers have died of wounds received in the military . . . .* (1836).

32. U.S., *An Act providing for the payment of the Invalid Pensioners.* (1789).

33. U.S., *An act more effectively to provide for the National Defence by establishing an Uniform Militia.* (1792). This law required circuit court judges to determine whether the disability of an applicant was acquired during the war, and if so, to assess its severity. What followed seems to anticipate the institution of judicial review: in letters to President Washington, Justices Jay and Iredell maintained that the statute was unconstitutional because its requirements were not judicial functions but duties belonging to the executive branch of government. Iredell also deemed the legislation violative because it would subject court decisions to revision or suspension by another branch of government. The letter to President Washington from Justice Jay and other members of the District Court of New York (communicated to Congress April 16, 1792) can be found on pp. 49–50 of Walter Lowrie and Walter Franklin's *American State Papers,* Vol. 1, *Miscellaneous.* The letter to President Washington from Justice Iredell and other members of the District Court of North Carolina, dated June 8, 1792, is on pp. 52–53 of that volume. A few months later, but without any formal consideration by the Supreme Court, a new law, *An Act to Regulate the Claims to*

Invalid Pensions (1793) resolved this issue of constitutional violation by calling for the establishment of State Pension Commissions.

34. U.S., *An Act Concerning Invalids.* (1794).

35. National pensions did not always succeed in saving Revolutionary War veterans from local charity. See, e.g., Philadelphia's *Alms House Admissions Book* and *Indenture Records* of 1785–1800, and its *Alms House Daily Occurence Docket* of 1789–1790.

36. U.S. House, J. Res. 16, Jan. 20, 1914.

37. U.S. Congressional Commission on National Aid to Vocational Education, *Hearings* pursuant to J. Res. 16. Published in conjunction with the Commission's report, June 1, 1914.

38. U.S. House, H. Doc. 1004. *Report* pursuant to J. Res. 16, p. 38.

39. In 1858, Sen. Morrill of Vermont proposed using federal money to establish colleges in the states. President Buchanan's veto claimed the bill violated state sovereignty. Four years later, President Lincoln reversed this action and signed the Land Grant College Act.

40. U.S. Congressional Commission on Vocational Education, *Report*, p. 33.

41. The bill was introduced as S. 703 by Sen. Hoke Smith, Chairman, Senate Committee on Education and Labor on Dec. 7, 1915, and as H.R. 11250, by Rep. Dudley Hughes, Chairman, House Committee on Education, on Dec. 16, 1915.

42. U.S. Congress, Sen. Carroll Page, *Congressional Record*, Vol. 53, p. 11472, July 24, 1916.

43. Ibid., Rep. Simeon Fess, Vol. 54, p. 174, Dec. 11, 1916.

44. Ibid., Rep. George Huddleston, p. 732, Dec. 22, 1916.

45. Ibid., Rep. Finis Garrett, p. 771, Jan. 2, 1917.

46. Ibid., Rep. Horace Towner, p. 716, Dec. 22, 1916.

47. Ibid., Rep. Frederick Dallinger, p. 722, Dec. 22, 1916.

48. Ibid., Sen. Carroll Page, Vol. 53, pp. 11466–11471, July 24, 1916.

49. Ibid., Rep. James Slayden, Vol. 54, p. 1079, Jan. 9, 1917.

50. U.S., *An Act to amend the Education of the Handicapped Act . . . .* (1975).

51. The Senate approved S. 703 on July 31, 1916; the House passed H.R. 11250 on Jan. 9, 1917. After a conference had resolved their disparities, President Wilson signed the act for promotion of vocational education on Feb. 23, 1917.

52. Seymour Sarason and John Doris, *Psychological Problems in Mental Deficiency,* p. 318.

53. U.S. House Committee on Education, *Report* introducing the bill proposed to provide vocational education. H. Report 597, p. 7.

54. U.S., *An Act to provide for vocational rehabilitation of disabled persons discharged from the military,* enacting clause. (1918).

55. Ibid., Sect. 2.

56. Federal Board for Vocational Education, *The Vocational Summary*, pp. 92–93.

57. U.S. House Committee on Rules, discussion pursuant to H. Res. 315, Oct. 9, 1919, p. 6.

58. U.S., *An Act to authorize the Establishment of a Bureau of War Risk Insurance in the Treasury Department.* (1914). Congress originally charged the Bureau with developing provisions to insure commercial shipping. The Soldiers and Sailors Insurance Law (1917) mandated that the Bureau should also compensate wounded soldiers.

59. Efforts to improve the Military Vocational Rehabilitation Act were begun by Rep. Simeon Fess (Report 31 from House Committee on Education to accompany H.R. 5225, June 10, 1919) and by Sen. William Kenyon (Report 2 from

Senate Committee on Education and Labor to accompany S. 1213, June 3, 1919).
The amending legislation was signed on July 11, 1919.

60. U.S., *An Act to provide for vocational rehabilitation of disabled persons discharged from the military,* Sect. 6. (1918).

61. Ibid., Sect. 4.

62. Federal Board for Vocational Education, *Annual Report,* 1919. Vol. 2, *Vocational Rehabilitation.*

63. Ibid., Table 17, p. 51.

64. U.S. House, H. Res. 315, Rep. John Rogers, Sept. 30, 1919.

65. U.S. House Committee on Rules, discussion of H. Res. 315, Oct. 9, 1919.

66. H. Res. 495 (66-2), Rep. Simeon Fess, Mar. 15, 1920.

67. H. Report 1105 pursuant to H. Res. 495, June 4, 1920.

68. Federal Board for Vocational Education, *Vocational Summary,* pp. 92–93.

69. E.g., Wilbert E. Fordyce, "Psychological Assessment and Management." There clearly are many individual exceptions to this pattern.

70. Marquis James, "A Debt of Honor Paid with a Worthless Check;" "A Pledge that Must be Redeemed."

71. Carolyn L. Vash, *The Psychology of Disability.*

72. U.S., *An act to provide for certain persons engaged in the land and naval service of the United States in the Revolutionary War.* (1818).

73. U.S., *An Act concerning Invalid Pensions,* Sect. 4. (1819).

74. Glasson, "Military Pension Legislation," p. 39.

75. U.S., *An Act to provide for certain persons engaged in the land and naval service of the United States, in the Revolutionary War.* (1818).

76. Glasson, "Military Pension Legislation," pp. 61–62.

77. Ibid., p. 113.

78. *New York Times,* 17:7, Mar. 30, 1921.

79. Ibid., 19:1, Apr. 6, 1921.

80. Ibid., 17:1, Apr. 7, 1921.

81. The bill was introduced in the Senate as S. 18 by Hoke Smith on May 20, 1919, and reported from the Senate Committee on Education and Labor on May 29, 1919 (S. Report 1). Rep. Simeon Fess introduced identical legislation in the House as H.R. 4438 on June 2, 1919. The House Committee on Education reported back the bill (H. Report 145) on July 23, 1919.

82. U.S., *An Act to provide for the promotion of vocational rehabilitation of persons disabled in industry,* enacting clause. (1920).

83. U.S. Congress, e.g., Rep. Anthony Griffin, *Congressional Record,* Vol. 59, p. 7599, May 25, 1920.

84. Ibid., Rep. William Green, Vol. 58, p. 6909, Oct. 14, 1919.

85. Ibid., Sen. Joseph Walsh, Vol. 59, p. 1382, June 19, 1919.

86. Ibid., Rep. Clyde Kelly, Vol. 58, p. 7028, Oct. 16, 1919.

87. U.S., *An Act to amend the Education of the Handicapped Act.* (1975).

88. U.S. Congress, Rep. Simeon Fess, *Congressional Record,* Vol. 58, p. 6914, Oct. 14, 1919.

89. Ibid., Rep. Clyde Kelly, p. 7028, Oct. 16, 1919.

90. Ibid., Rep. William Bankhead, p. 6909, Oct. 14, 1919.

91. Ibid., S. Report 1, May 29, 1919; H. Report 145, July 23, 1919.

92. Ibid., e.g., Rep. Carlos Bee, *Congressional Record,* Vol. 58, p. 6911, Oct. 14, 1919; Sen. William Kenyon, p. 512, June 2, 1919, and p. 1384, June 19, 1919.

93. Ibid., Sen. William King, p. 52, June 2, 1919.

94. U.S., *An Act to provide for the promotion of vocational rehabilitation of persons disabled in industry,* Sect. 2. (1920).

CHAPTER 3

Disability and Injury: Workmen's Compensation

After looking at the ways in which a speech by President Theodore Roosevelt and several theories of social behavior are related to the construction of disability, this chapter will focus on the disabling effects of workmen's compensation laws.[1] Specifying how these laws have led to the devaluation of people with physical handicaps bolsters the general argument that the disabling process in America is marked by a continuing interaction between society's laws and its prevailing attitudes.

We will see that a substantial part of the disability attendant upon compensation laws is related to their growth out of an earlier legal tradition. Their common law roots shaped laws that imposed extraordinary medical and legal constraints upon injured workers, and by creating for those workers an inferior social status, disabled them.

Two additional sets of disabling effects can be traced to the medical paradigm that is basic to workmen's compensation legislation. Its incorporation into law was probably the major source of the ideas that disability is an intra-individual attribute and that an equation exists between disability and injury. Furthermore, the paradigm seems to have led, indirectly but inexorably, to society's continuing disdain of those who are not gainfully employed.

By showing that these negative perceptions extended from injured workers to almost all handicapped people, this and the following chapter give the support of legislative history to Bogdan and Biklen's definition of "handicapism":

> a set of assumptions and practices that promote the differential and unequal treatment of people because of apparent or assumed physical, mental, or behavioral differences.[2]

A Peculiar Minority

As the speech cited below shows, President Theodore Roosevelt appeared to look at physically handicapped persons not as individuals, but
as members of a group that depends on the population as a whole. Because this relativistic view categorized people on the basis of character
and behavior (an expression of the Progressive impulses of the time), the
President's annual message of 1905 can probably be looked at as exem-
plifying a major source of disability. However, his words indicate the
presence of a second determinant of disability—one that centered on a
political mechanism unrelated to the period:

> Something can be done by legislation to help the general pros-
> perity; but no such help of a permanently beneficial character
> can be given to the less able and less fortunate, save as the re-
> sults of a policy which shall inure to the advantage of all indus-
> trious and efficient people who act decently; and this is only
> another way of saying that any benefit which comes to the less
> able and less fortunate must of necessity come even more to the
> more able and more fortunate.[3]

For although Roosevelt acknowledged, at least by implication, an interdependence of population segments, he also asserted the dependence of
the group made up of unfortunates. This creation of a population segment
to be dealt with only at the pleasure of the majority might have represented
his political sense of how best to deal with small numbers of people. As
such it points to government's ability to translate any statistical minority
into a political minority, and indicates that some part of the devaluation
of handicapped people may result from government fiat.

Defining "less fortunate" people as they are related to the majority
population probably points to a third root of disability. People with a
physical disorder are forced thereby to bear a special relationship to the
community, or in the language of Talcott Parsons,[4] to fill an identifiable
social role.

Parsons theorized that contemporary societies place occupants of the
"sick role" in a contractual relationship with the majority of the population. In great part the well-being of these occupants depends, or is
perceived to depend, upon the benevolence of society. But societal goods
are often given them with the expectation of one or another form of
repayment, and the fact that people with long-lasting or permanent physical disorders frequently are not sick appears to make little difference.
Moreover, as Theodore Roosevelt implied, these grants are generally

thought to benefit even more the ablebodied and decently behaving majority. Thus, looking at Roosevelt's message in the light of Parsons' theory suggests another instance in which the process of constructing disability does not directly depend upon society's views of human physical difference. Moreover, the very act of classifying handicapped people probably promotes disability by discouraging the ablebodied population from looking beyond the label of abnormality.

While the declared dependence of one segment of the population is both a sign and a source of its disability, society's perceptions of public beneficiary *qua* beneficiary are also part of the disabling process. A beneficiary of charity was often thought of as an object of charity. Depending upon the social and political conditions of the period, the meanings that society gave this object ranged from perpetual child to perpetual economic burden. No matter the political environment, however, this legislated depiction of an injured worker supported, and probably fostered, the view that persons who are objects are less than human—a view clarified by Edwin Schur's description of "objectification":

> Categorical devaluation implies treating people as objects. Others respond to the devalued persons in terms of their membership in the stigma-laden category. Individual qualities and actions become a secondary consideration. The stigmatized person is reacted to primarily as "an instance" of the category. At an extreme, he or she is viewed as having no other noteworthy status or identity. When that point is reached a person becomes—in the eyes of others—. . . *nothing but* "a delinquent," "a cripple," "a homosexual," "a black," "a woman." The indefinite article "a" underlines the depersonalized nature of such response. Members of the devalued category are treated as being virtually indistinguishable from, and in many respects substitutable for, one another.
>
> Stigmatized persons, then, are little valued *as persons*. Classificatory status tends to displace alternative criteria of personal worth. . . . others may claim license—implicitly if not explicitly—to treat the stigmatized individuals in exploitative and degrading ways.[5]

Another component of the devaluation generated by government grows out of the idea that physical impairment is synonymous with sin. As indicated by the many tales built on this notion, such beliefs remain active among a variety of groups. While these beliefs have almost certainly shaped thoughts about medically impaired people, they seem also to have shaped relevant political behavior. For example, Robert Crunden's 1982 book that discusses some of the achievements of the Progressive era in America,[6] indicates that one factor that helps to perpetuate these beliefs is the government conduct that already reflects these beliefs. Crunden argues that much political and social creativity of the time was guided by the moral rectitude inherent in Protestant orthodoxy. He concludes that health-related laws and agencies (he specifies the Food and Drug Administration) were developed because battling sickness was viewed as battling sin. Crunden's interpretation surely seems consistent with the social thought of the period. It is possible that the establishment of this agency can be explained in terms of economics rather than of religion. But even if this alternative explanation is not satisfactory, there is little doubt that acceptable government activity can support the beliefs that impose disability.

While Crunden did not write about disability or disability legislation, reasoning similar to his probably defined physical handicap as a problem to be solved by government intervention. Moreover, as indicated by the language of more recent legislation, Crunden's thesis suggests that defining disability in moral terms also decreases the likelihood of its being perceived as a socially determined construct.

Workmen's Compensation: Developmental Overview

Focusing on the comparability and comparative development of social security programs, two articles[7] by Vladimir Rys explain that such programs almost always include systems of caring for workers. Rys observes that national responses to the basic physical needs of citizens fall into two categories:

1. social insurance—by which he means that governments initiate (not merely regulate) and construct systems so that benefits are contributed to by, or on behalf of, the beneficiaries; and
2. social assistance—by which he means that governments provide for the physical needs of their citizens without the requirement that benefits be contingent upon specified contributions.

Rys's worldwide and historical surveys show that societies whose religious, political, and economic traditions value personal responsibility have often vigorously resisted schemes of social assistance. He further observes that national governments have usually, but not invariably, dealt with problems of human subsistence by first developing a program intended to benefit workers. Rys explains this variance in approach in terms of the fundamental political beliefs of the nation at issue—an explanation with implications for the United States.

Rys also states that the establishment of social security programs may be influenced by the actions of other nations, an assertion that receives quantitative support from a 1975 cross-national study by Collier and Messick.[8] These researchers selected "geographic proximity" and "language similarity" from the wide range of economic variables that they found related to the time of adoption. Then, by constructing patterns with these factors, Collier and Messick demonstrate diffusion of the concept of social security from one nation to another, as well as the effects of the more frequently studied *intra*national factors.[9]

They also find that new countries adopting social security arrangements often were less economically wealthy than were the countries that adopted similar programs earlier. By attributing this relationship to the "larger role of the state in later developing countries,"[10] Collier and Messick support Rys's assumption of a causal relationship between a nation's political ideology and the timing of the initiation of social insurance. In accordance with Rys's theory, the tenets of personal responsibility that are characteristic of American politics also account for the nation's emphasis on insurance rather than assistance. Furthermore, America's relatively late initiation of workmen's compensation laws may exemplify the country's tradition of noninterventionist government.

International impact on policy formation in the United States raises substantively and methodologically important questions. To address them here, however, would move the focus away from a concentration on American "disability legislation"—although available data would probably allow the comparisons necessary for such a study. While the problem of inter*state* diffusion[11] has special relevance to understanding legislative development in a federal nation, its analysis is also tangential to the purpose of this book. One can assume, however, that interstate diffusion in some part affected the sequence in which American compensation laws developed. In the case of Pennsylvania, for example, much of the language of the Compensation Act of 1915 is identical to that of the compensation laws of other states.[12]

Although the studies of Rys and of Collier and Messick each compare statutory definitions of injured beneficiaries, neither inquires specifically into legal definitions of physical handicap. That deficiency is shared by books that discuss the political and social activities of the period in which American compensation legislation was written[13]—a problem that requires analysis of primary sources to illuminate conceptions of disability.

Workmen's Compensation: American Beginnings

A systematic discussion of the legal doctrine of negligence is hardly central to the arguments of this book. Nevertheless, exploring the portion of common law that applied to employees can serve three useful purposes. First, such an inquiry can show that workmen's compensation legislation is part of the universal societal process of responding to change. Justice Sutherland's 1923 Supreme Court opinion implied this role:

> [T]he modern development and growth of industry, with the consequent changes in the relations of employer and employee, have been so profound in character and degree as to take away, in large measure, the applicability of the doctrines upon which rest the common-law liability of the master for personal injuries to a servant, leaving, of necessity, a field of debatable ground where a good deal must be conceded in favor of forms of legislation calculated to establish new bases of liability more in harmony with these changed conditions.[14]

Second, examining this area of common law helps to point out that the medical paradigm basic to compensation laws has almost inevitably led to a conception of disability as an intra-individual characteristic. An example of the operation of this paradigm can be found in the debates of the General Assembly that preceded Pennsylvania's first compensation statute.[15] Those debates implied that disability was nothing more than an inability to work because of injury. Third, the study of negligence law can show the factors, and their variable development, that disabled injured workers by placing them into a legal status different from that of other citizens.

Bias in Favor of Employers

In any common law action, the complainant can express his or her idea of the wrong suffered in the damages that are claimed. But, as specified below, because results of actions in common law almost always favored employers, this ability was often only an abstract exercise for the worker. For example, as long as any employer took "reasonable care" to make the work site and working conditions safe, the injured employee was without legal recourse, having assumed a job's "inherent risks."[16]

In addition to the disclaimer of inherent risk, two other available legal defenses also favored the employer. One expressed the principle of "contributory negligence." According to this traditional plea, if the slightest

blame could be attributed to the worker's actions, his employer was relieved of all responsibility for the injury. The second defense probably
derived from the feudal master/servant relationship. As was the custom
with this ancient system, courts considered a contract between employer
and employee immune to the actions of a third person. Therefore, a worker's injury that was in any degree the fault of a fellow employee excused
the employer from any legal guilt.

The efforts involved in establishing a justiciable case, and the time span
between introduction of litigation and final appeal of a judgment almost
surely caused financial strains for workers. It is likely too that the very
fact of bringing suit jeopardized their future employability. Moreover, even
if an employee were finally awarded damages, no legal mechanism assured
his collecting them.

The No-Fault Principle

Histories of compensation legislation by Rhodes and by Herman Miles
Somers and Anne Ramsay Somers[17] indicate that the development of publicly sponsored programs to aid the injured workers of industrialized nations was far from uniform. One way to follow these variations is to trace
one of the central principles of compensation law—dissociation of payment from fault.

Australia, New Zealand, Canada, and countries all over Europe developed laws incorporating this no-fault rule earlier than did the United
States. Consider, for example, the series of compulsory insurance programs instituted by the German government[18] during the 1880s. The state
compelled workers to insure themselves against sickness (one third of the
payments were to be contributed by their employers), directed employers
to compensate employees for death or for long-term disability without
regard to fault, and developed mandatory insurance for "old age and
invalidity." Like this complex of German laws, England's first compensation law,[19] enacted in 1897, provided for compensation of injured workers without regard to blame (except for those employees whose injuries
followed willful misconduct or intentional infliction). Statutory adoption
of this no-fault principle did erase some of the unfairness of relevant
common law. But because the English law of 1897 did not require employers to carry liability insurance, the actual payment of an award was
uncertain. However, both this problem of non-assured recovery of damages and the difficulty resulting from coverage limited to "hazardous
occupations" were eventually solved by legislative amendments.

Foreign laws probably exerted pressures on American legislatures to do for their citizens what other countries did for theirs. Nevertheless, American states did not enact no-fault compensation laws until the early 1900s, and the national employer liability law required proof of negligence until 1949.[20] The analyses by Rys and by Collier and Messick each imply that America's ethic of individualism was so profound as to resist international pressure.

A variety of efforts was made by the separate states to solve the problem of industrial injuries. The earliest state laws (1891–1907) did not contain a no-fault compensation principle but held employers directly liable for injuries to employees—apparently reflecting expectations that employers would pass on the expense as any other cost of production. According to an analysis in the January 1908 *Bulletin* of the Bureau of Labor,[21] several of these attempts at legislative relief were nothing more than restatements of existing common law.[22] However, other laws clearly abolished the "fellow-servant" defense, and some, holding fellow employees to be agents of the employer ("vice-principals"), charged the employer with liability for a worker's injury.[23] New York's statute (1902) was one of several that held the employer liable only if the fellow-worker at fault was a superintendent.[24] In New York's law, however, the employer's "inherent risk" defense also depended upon his compliance with mandated safety measures. Several other statutes helped to develop this new kind of law by forbidding contracts that required employees to waive their rights to sue.[25]

In sharp contrast to traditional negligence law, most of these "Employer Liability Statutes" placed the financial burdens of injury on employers. Within a few years, however, the no-fault mechanism was used to spread the liability of injury between owners and laborers. Perhaps this change in focus occurred because employers were generally able to seek political relief, or perhaps it came about because many Americans and their legislators believed that their nation's welfare depended on the welfare of employers. In any case, according to a 1917 research report of the National Industrial Conference Board, jurists in many states had begun to explain and justify compensation statutes with the understanding that an "[A]ccident originates . . . in the environment of production rather than in the conduct of the persons involved."[26] The authors of the report asserted that workmen's compensation laws of the several states "are intended to meet a public necessity, not a private wrong."[27]

But this principle seemed difficult for the federal government to accept. Under the aegis of the interstate commerce clause and the urging of President Theodore Roosevelt,[28] Congress wrote the first federal compensation law in 1906. The statute mandated that common carriers be liable to each employee for all damages resulting "from the negligence of any of its officers, agents, or employees or [from mechanical] defect or insufficiency due to its negligence."[29] The right to bring suit was preserved, the common law defenses of contributory negligence either by the injured employee or a fellow-servant were done away with, but financial compensation was still attached to the need to prove negligence.

In January 1908, a five to four decision by the Supreme Court[30] held the law unconstitutional because its language could be construed as encompassing employees not *directly* involved in interstate commerce. Congress revised the statute's ambiguous wording by the following April. Reflecting, or contributing to, a national atmosphere of industrial reform, the newly formulated law also specified the right to compensation if a common carrier violated "any statute enacted for the safety of employees. . . ."[31] A few years later this federal law also was judged to conform to the principles of due process and equal protection.[32] As previously noted, however, it was not for another forty years that the law compensated injured federal workers without the need for them to prove negligence.

The theme of no-fault compensation was first expressed in state legislation in Maryland's law of 1902.[33] Maryland established a "cooperative insurance fund" to be maintained by municipalities and by owners of mining, quarrying and railroading industries. This money was to be used by the state to compensate injured municipal employees and workers in these particularly hazardous industries, and was to be the injured employees' exclusive source of indemnity. In 1905, however, the Baltimore Court of Common Pleas found the law unconstitutional.[34] The court held that the statute deprived employers of property without due process of law, deprived employees of the right of trial by jury, and gave judicial powers to the administrating executive officers. The State of Maryland did not appeal the decision.

The principle of no-fault compensation was not found constitutional until courts considered a New Jersey statute of 1911.[35] Many states developed similar laws quickly thereafter,[36] and they were consistently approved in the many court challenges of the next several years. It was held in these frequent judicial confrontations[37] that choosing to be protected under workmen's compensation did not mean loss of an employee's right to trial by jury, that being forced to contribute to a state compensation fund did not deprive employers of property without due process, that exempting employers with fewer than five employees or exempting several occupational classes did not violate the equal protection clause, and that statutory adoption of the no-fault principle did not impair free contract.

Most states compelled both employers and employees to join in the compensation system. In the few states in which the system was elective, employers who refused acceptance were denied the common law defenses of "inherent risk," "contributory negligence," and "fellow servant." In Pennsylvania, for example, the system remained elective until 1974.[38]

Legislators and judges gradually adopted two related positions: (1) while precepts of common law may have been appropriate for earlier social conditions, current problems required a different complex of rules; and (2) development of these rules was within the prescribed powers of the states. State schedules based on injury and wage, and not on the plaintiff's evaluation of his wrong, now determined the size of an award. By 1913, twenty-four states, and by 1919, all but six states, had constitutional workmen's compensation laws. They each provided for ultimate rights of appeal on questions of law, were each administered by special state officers, and as an expression of principle, appeared to declare that a system assuring modest awards was socially more equitable than one in which collection of any damages was uncertain.

The Supreme Court explained and justified this system in an opinion written by Justice Pitney in 1916:

> The pecuniary loss resulting from the employee's death or disablement must fall somewhere. It results from something done in the course of an operation from which the employer expects to derive a profit. In excluding the question of fault as a cause of the injury, the act in effect disregards the proximate cause and looks to one more remote,—the primary cause, as it may be deemed,—and that is, the employment itself. For this both parties are responsible, since they voluntarily engage in it as co-adventurers.[39]

In a 1923 case Justice Sutherland translated Pitney's social reasoning into a statement of the legal theory basic to no-fault compensation:

> [W]orkmen's compensation legislation rests upon the idea of status, not upon that of implied contract; that is, upon the conception that the injured workman is entitled to compensation for an injury sustained in the service of an industry to whose operations he contributes his work as the owner contributes his capital—the one for the sake of the wages and the other for the sake of the profits. The liability is based, not upon any act or omission of the employer, but upon the existence of the relationship which the employee bears to the employment because of and in the course of which he has been injured.[40]

The temperate and reasoned language of each opinion, however, gave no inkling of the organizations of workers that had agitated for incorporating these principles of workmen's compensation into law. Neither did it suggest the number and multiple levels of court decisions needed to reach this new kind of law.

Despite these principles, though, it can be argued that the workmen's compensation system does not always or entirely exert its intended effects. For example, its frequently meager financial benefits have prompted a recent paper[41] to ask whether workmen's compensation laws fulfill the state's "interest in the prevention of pauperism. . . ."[42] Furthermore, an increasing awareness of causative links between disease and industrial conditions has probably led to views that the "exclusive remedy" of workmen's compensation is an inadequate remedy. Although by 1982 several states permitted workers the remedy of civil litigation as well as that of no-fault compensation,[43] forty-five states still prevented employees from suing their employers.

Workmen's Compensation: Medical and Psychological Considerations

It seems reasonable that legislative definitions of disability should depend upon the aims of the laws in which they are contained. However, despite this rather superficial variation, each American law that deals with handicapped people seems informed by a single belief: disability is a personal characteristic. The expression of this belief is especially evident in workmen's compensation laws, for these laws clearly regard disability as varying only with injury or disease. The increasing formalization of this concept of disability shows once more that much of America's disability-centered legislation has become a source of disability. And with this institutionalized relationship, it seems likely that in the case of legislative definitions, too, attention is diverted from the social causes of disability.

This intrapersonal concept of disability suggests that these laws derive from a medical model. To be sure, writers of workmen's compensation laws tried to modify or eliminate social sources of injury. But their attempts at achieving prevention and remedy were limited to the injuries themselves; they did not acknowledge that society might also modify the functional abilities of people who become injured. As a major argument in this book states, injured people become disabled to the extent that society diminishes these abilities.

This view that directs attention to the individual does not easily encourage a search for environmental causes of disability. Thus, if the medical paradigm continues to be used to shape law, disability will continue to be seen as the simple and direct result of physical defect, and there will be little or no inquiry into possible social remedies. (The earlier reference to the principle of individualism that guides so much American behavior may indicate why the medical paradigm is especially prominent in American legislation.) In the usual medical definition of disability, a focus on the individual seems consistent with that profession's therapeutic purposes. A similar focus in the law, however, probably has lessened the recognition that disability is socially determined. With workmen's compensation laws this perspective has certainly had identifiable disabling consequences.

The work of social psychologist Tamara Dembo offers a different understanding of this dimension of "location." In articles written over a period of several decades, Dembo has detached the concept of disability from the medically impaired individual by locating handicap in the interactions between ablebodied and physically defective people. A 1982 paper is particularly clear:

> handicapping conditions are *between* people, rather than *in* people. . . . Curiously enough, if the handicap is not *in* the person, then there are no handicapped persons. . . . handicapped people exist only in the eyes of a viewer. This places the handicap, as well as psychological rehabilitation, somewhere else than *within* the so-called handicapped person.[44]

While psychological analyses illustrate exogenous sources of disability, they discuss them only in the language of attitudinal or behavioral responses. Perhaps their failure to disavow the exclusivity of psychological reactions to the disabling process permits the facile inference that prevailing attitudes about human difference alone determine how a nation deals with the segment of its population that is handicapped. For example, several recent analyses[45] that label parts of the systems of education and occupation as disabling imply that the real determinants of these aspects of disability lie in the attitudes of ablebodied people. It seems important to attempt a broader explanation of disability by looking at such attitudes in the context of the theories and events that have generated American legislation.

Workmen's Compensation: Disabling Effects

This discussion of workmen's compensation legislation has pointed to its three major disabling consequences:

Disability and Non-Work

Workmen's compensation laws represented a new social mechanism with unknown economic ramifications. Perhaps it is therefore understandable that their construction called for modest rates of compensation—rates that were fractions of prior wages (generally one half to two thirds), and limited in aggregate dollars or in total time (often in both). It is also likely that these laws represented the concern for fiscal prudence that may have explained the half pay pensions for Revolutionary War veterans. From another perspective, however, relating compensation to the injured worker's prior wage may indicate that society's evaluation of injured people varies not only with the kind of occupation, but with its presence or absence.

If this latter interpretation holds, the often explicit religious syndrome of work, social value and moral worth seems to have emerged in, and been affirmed by, three legal implications: injury affects personal value, injury matters more to society when one has been paid more, and an injured person who has not worked is not valued at all. To the extent therefore that society measures a person's worth by his wage, these laws have perpetuated beliefs that inability to work, in the traditional sense of gainful employment, means diminished worth. Moreover, compensation schedules may have discouraged (or at least not encouraged) the view that disability varies with the roles played by physically impaired people.

Disability as Legal Status

The Federal Compensation Act of 1908 did not transfer awards to the estate of a worker for distribution according to his wishes.[46] In addition, the compensation statutes of most states awarded death benefits only if the worker had surviving dependents, and paid them only in accordance with a state-appointed trustee's assessment of their needs. Furthermore, most of these state laws also arranged to estimate abilities of injured workers. Arizona's statute, for example, specified that a recovering worker was to receive one half the difference between his previous wage and "the average amount he is earning or is capable of earning."[47] Laws such as this implied indirectly that because "disability" was simply related to gainful employment, it should be a subject of state laws that deal with employment.

Although each statute included some provision for initial medical care, not one offered what appears to be genuine medical care—that which depends only on medical needs. "Care" was limited in days or weeks, was restricted by financial cost, or was directly related to the worker's wage prior to his injury. Several states (for example, Kansas, New Hampshire, and New York)[48] paid for immediate medical care only if the worker died and left no dependents. States found it within their authority not only to assess the abilities of injured workers, but to define the needs of those individuals (and their families) whose injuries precluded or limited their ability to work.

The employment status that Justice Sutherland used to explain this body of legislation seems to have become for injured employees one of legally proclaimed lesser status. Because of that differentiation, although many portions of workmen's compensation laws have been judged to be constitutional, questions arise about their violation of the Constitution's equal protection clause. Furthermore, as far as legislative actions initiate or confirm personal prejudices, that particular status probably led to a legally validated social devaluation.

Disability as Physical Defect

As with the earlier employer liability statutes, state-to-state variations characteristic of the American federal system existed. Compensation laws varied in the monetary value they attached to injury, in their lists of compensable injuries, and in the exactness with which they expected degrees of partial disability to be determined. For example, California expected differences in "partial disabilities" to be determined with the precision of a single percentage point. Similarly, a hand in New Jersey was, in law, worth less than a hand in Wisconsin.

However, common themes also existed in compensation legislation. The laws of almost all states exempted agricultural, household, and "casual" employees. Each statute denied compensation to any employee whose injury was deliberate, and most, to those who were intoxicated at the time of injury. Apparently in the name of fairness and free choice, each jurisdiction allowed both the employee and the employer to have a physician evaluate impairment.

The most striking constant, though, was the legal conception of disability. With the single exception discussed below, each state defined disability as a loss of ability to work caused by an injury sustained "in the course of or arising out of employment."[49] Relating injury to work is surely appropriate to laws that deal with workers. But by labeling injured workers as disabled, these laws failed to distinguish between the handicap of injury and the handicap imposed upon people with injuries.

The problem of second injuries also illumines the conceptual weakness of defining disability as nothing more than the result of an injury. For example, several statutes mandated that the maximum scheduled amount was to be paid when an injury transformed a pre-existing physical disorder into a total disability. But these laws actually diminished the likelihood that anyone with a pre-existing injury would secure employment. For example, when Somers and Somers[50] write of the one-eyed Oklahoma worker whose injury cost his remaining eye, they expose as fiction the legislated proclamation that workers with pre-existing physical disorders were as free to work as their ablebodied co-workers. According to the state's law, the worker was compensated for "total disability," and within a few days, across the nation, 7,000 workers with one eye, one arm, or one leg were fired. "Second injury clauses" subsequently became part of almost all statutes. These modifications made compensable only that portion of lost physical function judged to result from a new injury.

Even though laws were changed, many employers apparently continued to consider hiring people with physical impairments as an unnecessary financial risk. While some component of such behavior was undoubtedly a rational response to lack of knowledge of statutory changes, some portion surely represented the power of devaluating assumptions.

Only California's 1913 law hinted, with a single clause, at a different concept of disability:

> In determining the percentages of permanent disability, account shall be taken of the nature of the physical injury or disfigurement, the occupation of the injured employee and his age at the time of the injury.[51]

This portion of the law indicates recognition that exactly the same injuries did not necessarily produce the same effects in, for example, a railroad switchyard worker and an office manager, or a twenty-year-old and a sixty-year-old. According to Somers and Somers' history of workmen's compensation, however, most workers were angered and mystified by this clause, and its subjectivity and complexity made for difficult administration.[52] The report is hardly surprising when the criteria of a single law deviate to such a great degree from those that are generally accepted.

Nevertheless, this legislative fragment does represent a statutory attempt to define disability as something that varied with factors other than severity of injury. The clause hints at an ecological conception of disability in which environmental as well as personal factors are determinative. But perhaps the experience with this law indicates that because disability varies with each person, physically handicapped individuals do not always fit into the legislative categories that seem to develop from a medical paradigm.

Such rigid categories are exemplified by the definitions referred to in a 1967 presentation of a survey method for identifying disabled Americans.[53] In this article, Lawrence Haber of the Social Security Administration distinguishes two sets of definitions used by government. He points out that agencies charged with awarding monetary benefits tend to focus directly on medical impairments, while agencies whose aim is rehabilitation look as well at the individual's potential for employment, a process that requires assessing, or at least recognizing, personality characteristics.

Two examples that support Haber's observation follow. First, the Social Security Act Amendments of 1952 define as disabled those people who are unable

> to engage in any substantial gainful activity by reason of any
> medically determinable physical or mental impairment which can
> be expected to be permanent.[54]

And the 1966 Education of the Handicapped Act states that

> the term "handicapped children" means mentally retarded, hard
> of hearing, deaf, speech impaired, visually handicapped, seri-
> ously emotionally disturbed, crippled, or other health impaired
> children who by reason thereof require special education and re-
> lated services.[55]

Subsequent revisions[56] of that act contain similar definitions.

Although the definitions cited below do indicate that Haber's division no longer holds, the paradigmatic basis of the laws seems unchanged. The Rehabilitation Act of 1973 considers disabled

> any individual who (A) has a physical or mental disability which
> for such individual constitutes or results in substantial handicap
> to employment and (B) can reasonably be expected to benefit in
> terms of employability from vocational rehabilitation services.[57]

In 1974 Congress amended this law so that the definition of disability no longer centered on employability, or on an official judgment of potential success in the rehabilitative services offered by government. The Act then defined as disabled

> any person who A) has a physical or mental impairment which

substantially limits one or more of such person's major life activities, B) has a record of such impairment, or C) is regarded as
having such an impairment.[58]

Because this amendment acknowledged a range of functions, the democratic promise of equal legal opportunity seems to have become more
certain. But even though this definition reflected considerable political
change in America, the legal conception of disability remained that of an
entity located within the individual.

Moreover, while later laws have related disability to the roles of student
or employee (or in the case of the amended Rehabilitation Act, to a variety
of unspecified roles), they have reflected a conception of disability as a
measurement of performance. None has conceived, instead, of disability
as *being measured by* the roles to be performed, so that disability might
be more or less or present or absent when a medically impaired person
occupies a particular role.

Notes

1. States that prohibit discrimination on the basis of gender now refer to these
statutes as Workers' Compensation Laws. The terminology in this book will be
that used in the period under discussion.
2. Robert Bogdan and Douglas Biklen, "Handicapism," p. 14.
3. Theodore Roosevelt, *The Works of Theodore Roosevelt,* Vol. XVII, p. 316.
Annual message of 1905.
4. Talcott Parsons, *The Social System,* esp. "Deviant Behavior and the Mechanisms of Social Control," pp. 249–325.
5. Edwin M. Schur, *Labeling Women Deviant: Gender, Stigma and Social
Control,* pp. 30–31.
6. Robert M. Crunden, *Ministers of Reform: The Progressives' Achievement
in American Civilization, 1889–1920.*
7. Vladimir Rys, "The Sociology of Social Security;" "Comparative Studies
of Social Security: Problems and Perspectives."
8. David Collier and Richard E. Messick, "Prerequisites Versus Diffusion:
Testing Alternative Explanations of Social Security Adoption."
9. Explaining the development of any social institution by analyzing only the
sociological factors internal to a nation ignores the effects of cross-national diffusion. The questionable methodological validity inherent in this approach has
been defined as "Galton's Problem." According to Collier and Messick ("Prerequisites"), most studies follow either of two theoretical approaches to understanding the development of a nation's social security: the "Prerequisites Theory,"
which focuses on *intra*national determinants, or the "Diffusion Theory," which
focuses on the spread of causative factors *among* nations. If a purpose of cross-
national research is to understand the interaction of causative factors within nations as well as among nations, then credence can only be given studies that follow
either theory with due regard to its dependence on the other.
10. Collier and Messick, "Prerequisites," p. 1301.
11. E.g., Jack L. Walker, "The Diffusion of Innovations Among the American
States."

12. In the several years prior to the passage of Pennsylvania's 1915 workmen's compensation law (Commonwealth of Pennsylvania, *Act. No. 338*), the governor established commissions to study the structure and effects of this kind of legislation in other states.

13. E.g., Edward A. Ross, *Seventy Years of It;* George Mowry, *The Era of Theodore Roosevelt;* Richard Hofstadter, ed., *The Progressive Movement: 1900– 1915; Richard Hofstadter, The Age of Reform: From Bryan to F.D.R..*

14. *Cudahy Packing Co. v. Parramore,* at p. 423. This case affirmed that injuries acquired on the way to work arose from employment and were therefore compensable under state law.

15. *Pennsylvania Legislative Journal, House,* Vol. IV, p. 4164, May 20, 1915.

16. It is well known that American industrialized regions are often characterized by occupational competition and consequent social immobility. The individual choice implied by the principle of "inherent risk" seems incongruous with these constraints.

17. J. E. Rhodes, 2nd, *Workmen's Compensation;* H. M. Somers and A. R. Somers, *Workmen's Compensation: Prevention, Insurance and Rehabilitation of Occupational Disability.*

18. The compulsory legislation of Germany was begun in 1884, and added to each year through 1887. See Rhodes, *Workmen's Compensation,* pp. 42–53.

19. Because the English law was elective and involved courts and private insurance programs in its administration, it may have been especially influential on the U.S. This point is made in Somers, *Workmen's Compensation,* p. 30.

20. U.S., *An Act to amend . . . "An Act to provide compensation for employers of the United States . . .".* (1949).

21. Pertinent sections of the laws are printed in the U.S. Bureau of Labor, *Bulletin,* no. 74. Page references in the four following notes are to that *Bulletin.*

22. E.g., Georgia, *Code of 1895* (pp. 59–60); North Dakota, *Revised Codes of 1905, Acts of 1907* (pp. 77–78).

23. E.g., Territory of Arizona, *Revised Statutes of 1901* (p. 55); Wisconsin, *Annotated Statutes of 1898* (pp. 89–90).

24. E.g., New York, *Acts of 1902, Acts of 1906* (pp. 74–76); Ohio, *Acts of 1902, Acts of 1904* (pp. 78–80).

25. E.g., Iowa, *Code of 1897 & Suppl. of 1902, Acts of 1907* (pp. 62–63); Colorado (p. 57).

26. National Industrial Conference Board, *Workmen's Compensation Acts in the United States: The Legal Phase,* p. 3.

27. Ibid., p. 4.

28. Theodore Roosevelt, *Works,* Vol. XVII, p. 422. Annual message of 1906.

29. U.S., *An Act Relating to liability of common carriers . . . .* (1906).

30. The court reached this judgment after hearing two cases together: *Howard v. Ill. C. R.* and *Brooks v. Southern P. Co.*

31. U.S., *An Act Relating to the liability . . . .* (1908).

32. *New York Central R. Co. v. White* tested both New York's compensation law and the Federal Compensation Act of 1908. Finding the no-fault compensation principle to comply with the due process and equal protection clauses probably facilitated favorable judgments in e.g., *Phila., B'more and Wash. R. Co. v. Schubert; Central R. of New Jersey v. Colasurdo; Erie R. Co. v. Welsh; Shanks v. Delaware L. and W. R. Co.*

33. Maryland, *Acts of 1902.* Reprinted in U.S. Bureau of Labor, *Bulletin* no. 45, March 1903, pp. 400–06.

34. *Franklin v. United Railways and Electric Co. of Baltimore.*

35. New Jersey, *Acts of 1911,* Ch. 95.

36. As discussed in *Bulletin of U.S. Bureau of Labor Statistics*, no. 126, pp. 9–130.

37. Right to jury trial: *New York Central R. Co. v. White;* Due process: *Jeffrey Mfg. Co. v. Blagg; New York Central R. Co. v. White; Mountain Timber Co. v. State of Washington;* Arbitrary classification: *Northern Pacific R. v. Meese;* Impaired contract: *Hawkins v. Bleakly.*

38. Pennsylvania, *An Act Amending [the liability Act of 1915], Act. No. 263,* P.L. 782 (1974).

39. *New York Central R. Co. v. White,* at p. 205.

40. *Cudahy Packing Co. v. Parramore,* at p. 423.

41. *Report of the National Commission on State Workmen's Compensation Laws.*

42. This justification was pronounced in *New York Central R. Co. v. White,* at p. 207.

43. Debra McCloskey Barnhart, "The Dual Capacity Doctrine: Piercing the Exclusive Remedy of Workers' Compensation." California, Illinois, Michigan, Montana, and Ohio have adopted a "dual capacity doctrine" that views employers not only in an employment relationship, but also as suppliers of goods and services. Their employees are not restricted to the remedy of compensation but may also bring suit as consumers.

44. Tamara Dembo, "Some Problems in Rehabilitation as Seen by a Lewinian," p. 133. In her work in rehabilitation psychology, Dembo has developed a "topological" theory of handicap to treat physically impaired individuals. I have tried to use a similar theory in the context of *collective* social actions.

45. E.g., Gary T. Athelstan, ed., *The Disabled Worker: Overcoming the System's Barriers;* Nettie Bartel and Samuel Guskin, "A Handicap as a Social Phenomenon;" Evelyn Deno, "Special Education as Developmental Capital."

46. The federal liability acts provide for payment to the "personal representative" of the decedent.

47. Arizona, *Acts of 1913,* Ch. VII, Sect. 72 (2), reprinted in U.S. Bureau of Labor, *Bulletin* no. 74, p. 183.

48. U.S. Bureau of Labor, *Bulletin* no. 126: Kansas, *Acts of 1911,* Ch. 218, Sect. 14 (p. 257); New Hampshire, *Acts of 1911,* Ch. 163, Sect. 6(c) (p. 326); New York, *Consolidated Laws,* Ch. 31, Sect. 1207(c) (p. 338).

49. Language common to the workmen's compensation statutes of many states.

50. Somers, *Workmen's Compensation,* p. 135 n. 81.

51. California, *Acts of 1913,* Ch. 176, Sec. 15 (7).

52. Somers, p. 72 and n.43.

53. Lawrence D. Haber, "Identifying the Disabled: Concepts and Methods in the Measurement of Disability."

54. U.S., *An Act to amend title II of the Social Security Act. . . .* (1952), p. 771.

55. U.S., *An Act to strengthen . . . assistance for . . . schools . . . .* (1966), p. 1204.

56. E.g., U.S., *An Act to extend . . . assistance to schools . . . .* (1970); *An Act to amend the Education of the Handicapped Act . . . .* (1975).

57. U.S., *An Act to Replace the Vocational Rehabilitation Act* (1973), p. 361.

58. U.S., *An Act to extend the . . . Rehabilitation Act of 1973 . . . .* (1974), p. 1619.

CHAPTER 4

Disability and Charity: Rehabilitation for Civilians

This chapter and the next will show that disabling social policies can in large part be traced to institutionalized practices of charity and segregation. In this chapter that process is demonstrated by presenting the legislative background of federally sponsored rehabilitation. Chapter 5 discusses the same method of constructing disability in the context of education.

First, in order to specify antecedents of the belief that biological deficiency confers social deficiency, several colonial laws are examined. Then, after a discussion of Social Darwinism, the chapter will consider some disabling effects of the institution of charity.

A final segment shows that the Vocational Rehabilitation Act of 1920 furthered the development of disability by its implication that only people who contributed to the nation's economic welfare were worthy of assimilation. That even these "worthy" people were viewed as inherently inadequate, however, is evidenced by their frequent restriction to relatively menial work. The circular mechanism basic to the self-fulfilling prophecy indicates that these vocational constraints and negative perceptions about the natural, inherent, competence of handicapped people probably reinforced one another.

Analyses of the unemployment of ablebodied workers offer another useful perspective on this problem of denying the abilities of the physically handicapped population. Consider, for example, this portion of a 1922 discussion of labor problems by Gordon Watkins:

> Unemployment not only tends to dishearten the workers, but
> also fill them with resentment against the present industrial or-
> der. Discontent and a tendency to radicalism are the natural

consequences of unemployment. . . . Unemployment, moreover, is probably the greatest single factor in breeding social unrest. Revolutionary philosophy finds fertile soil in the minds of those who are able and willing to work but who, on account of conspicuous weaknesses in our economic system, are forced to accept idleness with its train of cumulative indebtedness, want, and misery.[1]

It seems likely that the intra-individual tensions and social alienation that Watkins attributes to unemployment can also occur when society assigns handicapped people to malemployment or to idleness. This possibility is one more reason for formulating public policies that treat handicapped citizens only as differently as their physical impairments require, and not so differently as to create a politically inferior population segment.

Roots of Disability in Colonial Legislation

In 1665, the Duke of York governed much of the territory that now comprises portions of New York, Pennsylvania, New Jersey, and Delaware. By assigning the treatment of physically handicapped citizens to private charity, the "Duke's Laws" began to formalize the link between handicap and poverty. When one reads these laws after looking at later legislation, they appear to contain two significant sources of disability.

The first of these can be traced to the earliest portion of the Duke's Laws—a portion that identified charity as a function of government:

> That every Inhabitant within this Government shall contribute to all Charges, both in Church and Coloney; whereof he doth or may receive benefit, and every such Inhabitant that doth not voluntarily Contribute proportionately to his Ability, with the rest of the same Towne to all Common Charges both Civill and Ecclesiasticall, shall be compelled thereunto by Assessment and Distress to be Levied by the Constable.[2]

In 1748–49 the Province of Pennsylvania formalized this relationship by transforming private philanthropists into government workers:

> And be it further enacted . . . That the said overseers of the poor for the several townships, city and boroughs . . . shall forever hereafter in name and in fact be and they are hereby declared to be bodies politic and corporate in law to all intents and purposes.[3]

The Duke's Laws' arrangements for care of "Distracted Persons" continued this theme by suggesting that a connection between charity and physical handicap was a necessary by-product of the connection between charity and government:

> That in regard the Condition of Distracted Persons may Prove of
> Publique Concerne, and for that it is too greate a burthen for
> one Towne allone to beare, It may be taken into Consideration
> at the Assizes whether the other townes of that riding ought not
> to Contribute to the Charge.[4]

The disabling force of legitimizing this connection will be demonstrated by inquiring into the methods and emphases of organized charities. Another form of disability—a legalized inequality of treatment under the law—can probably be traced to the denial of public responsibility that is implied by official willingness to place care of citizens in private hands.

The second major aspect of disability that can be traced to the Duke's Laws concerns society's practice of associating indigence and physical defect. Although this association obviously has many determinants, the view that handicapped people should be looked on as beneficiaries of public generosity was stated very early in the Duke of York's provisions for electing overseers to care for the poor:

> That For the making and proportioning the Levies and Assess-
> ments for building and repairing the Churches, Provision for the
> poor, maintenance for the Minister; as well as for the more or-
> derly managing of all Parochiall affairs in other Cases exprest,
> Eight of the most able Men of each Parish be by the Major part
> of the Householders of the said Parish Chosen to be Overseers.[5]

Subsequent laws developed special mechanisms to deal with "other Parochiall affairs." But often, at least in Pennsylvania,[6] overseers were chosen to direct the care of *the indigent as well as the infirm.* (According to Heffner's history of "poor relief,"[7] similarly designated overseers continued into the twentieth century.) The earliest law of the Province of Pennsylvania declared that those who were physically infirm should be dealt with as paupers—as recipients of alms:

> all persons falling into decay, want or poverty, upon their com-
> plaint made to the justices of the peace and overseers of the
> poor of the respective counties where such decayed or indigent
> persons shall happen to be or reside, the justices of the peace

and overseers of the poor shall take due care to relieve such
poor and indigent persons.[8]

Perhaps because a number of statutes dealt with physically handicapped
people and indigent people as a single group, the spatial and social dis-
tance imposed upon paupers extended to "the physically impotent."

This legislative process of generalizing negative beliefs about paupers
to handicapped people has continued for centuries. Solicitation of gifts of
real property for use by the poor[9] that were made by Pennsylvania's Assembly Session of 1748–49 can be found in almost identical language in
the vocational rehabilitation laws of 1918 and 1920.[10]

One section of a 1705 statute charged family members with the support
of physically handicapped people:

> And be it further enacted by the authority aforesaid, That the
> father and grandfather and the mother and grandmother and the
> children of every poor, old, blind, lame, and impotent person, or
> other poor person not able to work, being of a sufficient ability,
> shall at their own charges relieve and maintain every such poor
> person as the justices of the peace at their general quarter-ses-
> sion shall order and direct, on pain of forfeiting forty shillings
> for every month they shall fail therein.[11]

The demand that handicapped people be cared for by their families may
express disparate, and perhaps co-existing, motives: a concern for conserving public money, a desire to assure the best care, and a belief that
families are primarily responsible for their members. Possibly the statute
also embodies the view that separation from the general community is a
natural condition for the handicapped population. But no matter the determinants, such legislative mandates almost surely shaped the predispo-
sitions that imposed segregation and social marginality on physically
defective people.

Another statute added a different dimension to the legislated identity
between the impotent and the poor:

> And to the end that the money raised only for the relief of such
> as are impotent and poor may not be misapplied and consumed
> by the idle, sturdy and disorderly beggars:
> Be it further enacted by the authority aforesaid, That every
> such person . . . shall upon the shoulder of the right sleeve of the
> upper garment of every such person, in an open and visible

manner, wear such badge or mark as is hereinafter mentioned
and expressed: (That is to say) a large Roman P.[12]

This visible sign was never mentioned again. One purpose for such a
system of identification may have been the prevention of fraud. Possibly,
too, the practice of identifying recipients of charity may have been used
to promote a socially desired goal of philanthropy. Nonetheless, proclaiming the dependence of handicapped individuals on the donations of the
majority, especially so egregiously by a badge, is clearly disabling.

Two laws of the Province of Pennsylvania defined physically infirm
people as causes for legal action, thereby imposing a distinctive (and therefore, disabling) status upon them. One of these statutes, after specifying
"what settlement shall render one an inhabitant,"[13] declared that if illegal
residents who became indigent could not be returned to the place of their
last legal settlement, the Province of Pennsylvania was to be indemnified
by the county of origin. The second law permitted litigation by individuals
if handicapped servants were foisted upon them:

> [Be it enacted that every person] who shall import and sell or
> dispose of any servants who at the time of such sale were with
> child or afflicted with such secret or other diseases as shall ren-
> der them incapable of performing the ordinary and reasonable
> duties of servants, . . . persons so disposing of or selling such
> servant or servants shall be liable to answer the purchaser or
> purchasers all damages which he, she or they shall sustain . . . in
> any court of record within this province.[14]

Although neither law specifies handicap, the use of "infirm" and "impotent" in other laws of the period make it seem reasonable that these
statutes also included physically handicapped people.

The legislative sessions of 1729–30 enacted a series of laws "to dis-
courage the great importation and coming in of numbers of foreigners
and of lewd, idle and ill-affected persons."[15] The laws applied especially
rigid exclusionary mandates to those who were visibly ill (and perhaps
also to those with visible physical impairments). One statute arranged for
the good behavior of convicts to be secured by a bond of five pounds,[16]
but demanded that persons who are physically handicapped are not merely
to be paid for or vouched for, but are to be deported:

> [The] mayor, recorder and aldermen . . . shall and may compel
> the said master, merchant or importer of . . . infant, lunatic,
> maimed, aged, impotent or vagrant person or persons to give

sufficient security to carry and transport such . . . person or persons to the place or places from whence such person or persons were imported.[17]

The unfavorable comparison of handicapped people to felons probably served to legitimate the expectation that the morality of physically impaired people is defective. Furthermore, the frequent association in law of aliens and people who are physically impaired may have extended notions of undesirability from one group to the other. Pehaps because handicap was so often seen in this legal framework, the mystery and fearfulness prompted by strangeness became part of perceptions of physical difference.

It is understandable that there was a need for able bodies in the growing province. But by formalizing ideas that physical ability is central to social worth, these laws established a rationale for treating handicapped people without regard to such a need. For example, this idea probably informs the later practice of segregating school children with physical handicaps without any relation to their educational needs. If handicapped people were thought of as useless as well as alien, mysterious, and dangerous, demands for their exclusion do not seem surprising.

Converting physically dependent people to socially dependent people is not entirely based on fears of danger or calculations of cost effectiveness. This suggestion may have its root in another portion of the Duke's Laws:

> For as much as the good Management of the Militia is the Support of all Governments in Peace and Safety, to which all Persons of what quality soever are obliged in duty & Conscience in their proportions to be Aiding and Assisting to this good end these following Lawes are to be observed.
>
> 1. First, that every Male Person above the age of sixteen years Except, Justices, Sherriffes, high Constables and under Sherriffe Petty Constable Ministers and professed School-masters, Physicians and Chirurgeons, allowed of by two Justices, Clarkes of Assizes or Sessions Publique Notaries, Masters of Shipps or vessels above Twenty Tunns Constant heardsmen or *such as for bodily Infirmity* or old age shall be excused by the Justices in any Sessions. [my emphasis][18]

The assertion that physical infirmity and military service are incompatible appears to have been questioned only once. The Revolutionary Army's Corps of Invalids (discussed in Chapter 2) suggests that at that time the nation's need for experts was so critical that wounded soldiers were given the opportunity to be useful. At every other time in the country's history, however, "infirmity" has precluded any contribution to the military. This absolute limitation indicates that even at this early stage a medical paradigm informed the social decisions that resulted in "disability legislation."

The repeated laws that forbade handicapped people from defending their country appear to express a continuing concern about the nation's economic welfare. Surely, many of the early laws that dealt with handicapped soldiers reflected collective economic considerations. And the law providing for vocational rehabilitation of soldiers after the War of 1914–1918 was probably justified by prospects of the nation's economic health. But the modern army's refusal to enlist a paraplegic teacher, for example, indicates that this concern is not entirely genuine. The publicly acceptable language of economic concern may hide an uneasiness with (or frank disdain of) physical difference that has become increasingly publicly *un*-acceptable. But, as is so often argued here, such uneasiness is not always or entirely an expression of natural, visceral, fear. Evidence often indicates that negative feelings about people with physical abnormalities are in great part the result of social construction.

One reason for this weakened connection between assimilation and potential productivity may be rooted in the institution of charity. The next section begins to illustrate part of the disabling power of organized charities by discussing the intellectual context of their formation.

Social Darwinism

Social Darwinism dominated American social thought during the period in which charitable agencies became organized. The eugenics movement suggests that the theory articulated existing beliefs, however vague, that physically handicapped people threaten the survival of the human species. But in one sense the theory was also alien to American thought, for it was antithetic to the nation's tradition of caring for those unable to care for themselves. There is little doubt that the translation of Social Darwinism into practice, and thus the prevalence of philanthropic activity, depends upon the political and economic climate of the period. However, it will become clear that the connections between charity and disability are often independent of the currency of Social Darwinism.

Richard Hofstadter's *Social Darwinism in American Thought*[19] attributes the scholarly and popular acceptance of Herbert Spencer's social theories to the same adherence to rationalism that accounted for America's rapid adoption of Darwin's biological theory. However, Spencer's *Social Statics*[20] contains such a critical weakness that his ideas do not *explain* human behavior. (This is not to say, though, that because the acceptability of these ideas is so sensitive to political events, they do not *influence* human behavior.) Asserting that "[A]ll imperfection is unfitness to the conditions of existence," Spencer blamed cases of *maladaptation to society exclusively on the defective characteristics* of individual human beings.

Moreover, Spencer believed that the eventual disappearance of deficient faculties was "an essential principle of life." This doctrine permitted him to argue that "humanity must in the end become completely adapted to its conditions. . . ."[21] His vision of naturally determined societal progress apparently compelled him to label efforts at shaping society as interference with natural law. As a consequence, Spencer generally condemned attempts to fit defective individuals into society. Because such pursuits enabled "the recipients to elude the necessities of our social existence,"[22] Spencer believed that charity disrupted, or at least impeded, the natural progression of human society.

Nevertheless, he did praise two attributes of *private* charity, asserting the efficacy of "all assuagings of distress instigated by sympathy; for . . . charity is in its nature essentially civilizing."[23] He also found value in that particular form of charity "which may be described as helping men to help themselves," for

> in helping men to help themselves, there remains abundant scope
> for the exercise of a people's sympathies. . . . And, although by
> these ameliorations the process of adaptation must be remotely
> interfered with, yet in the majority of cases, it will not be so
> much retarded in one direction as it will be advanced in
> another.[24]

From one perspective, Spencer anticipates the concept of rehabilitation when he wrote of that charity "which may be described as helping men to helping themselves." However, in America the long history of beliefs that the nation should not assimilate people who appeared to lack economically productive abilities seems to have altered the phrase to "helping *some* men to help themselves."

Although Spencer did not revise the substance of *Social Statics* after its initial publication in 1851, the preface to the first American edition of 1864 indicates a developing certainty about charity's value:

> I would bring into greater prominence the transitional nature of
> all political institutions, and the consequent *relative* goodness of
> some arrangements which have no claim to *absolute* goodness.[25]

While his view of the worth of charity evidently changed, at least to the point that private philanthropy could be justified, Spencer continued to believe that the only function of the state was to protect the rights of its citizens.[26] His idea that providing relief for one class necessarily infringed upon the rights of another led to his assertion that charity sponsored by government both interfered with the natural process of social adaptation and represented an illegitimate and immoral exercise of power.

Prior to the publication of *Social Statics*, no level of American government directly sponsored programs of welfare. Several factors may account for this fact. Considerable evidence suggests that many people in America envisioned the nation's welfare as dependent on each citizen's ability to work. Moreover, perceptions of the nation's need for material productivity might have subordinated the view that assuring the subsistence of individuals may give them the time and energy to become productive. But perhaps the most plausible explanation centers on the American expectation of personal responsibility, for the tradition of individualism developed by the pragmatic needs of the colonies, by the Protestant work ethic, and by Jeffersonian conceptions of government obligation, almost certainly helped to foster beliefs that the welfare of handicapped people was a private problem.

Of the several objections to Spencer's views, that of the prominent botanist William Bateson is decidedly relevant to the idea of social construction that is at the core of this book. Bateson's observations had convinced him that one could not explain biological behavior and social conduct by the same mechanism:

> I have seen . . . the claim put forward that the teaching of biological science sanctions a system of freest competition for the means of subsistence between individuals, under which the fittest will survive and the less fit tend to extinction. That may conceivably be a true inference applicable to forms which, like the thrushes, live independent lives, *but so soon as social organization begins,* the competition is between societies and not individuals. [my emphasis][27]

Comparison of the behavior of animals with the conduct of human communities is probably the essential feature of Spencer's theory. His belief that "under the natural order of things society is constantly excreting its unhealthy, imbecile, slow, vacillating, faithless members"[28] appears to have meant to him that human society and animal species conformed to the same law of evolution and to the same mechanism of natural selection.

In contrast to Spencer's unyielding analogy, though, Bateson's biologically grounded objection indicates that the actions of a society composed of human beings in some part depends on the variable of organization. The correlation between power and organization implicit in his objection offers a theme for a general analysis of political behavior. But of specific pertinence to this book, Bateson's comments point to a mechanism that enables America's majority population to determine the social position of physically handicapped individuals. In more general terms, Bateson's objection indicates that the ability of human beings to function within their societies is in large part a social product.

It is interesting to note, though, that even though Bateson viewed cultural organization as a determinant of human behavior, he used pure Mendelian genetics to explain the mechanics of mental retardation. The extensive discussion of eugenics by Sarason and Doris[29] reports that Bateson's adoption of hereditarian theories of mental retardation led him to call for the sterilization of persons with mental deficiencies. He believed people with mental retardation were not only genetic products but genetic threats. But despite this expression of what was a conventional view at the time, Bateson's criticism of the careless use of Mendel's theory as a basis for Social Darwinism is similar to the holding that disability is a social product and a social threat.

Spencer's writings seem to have articulated the theoretic justification for American legislative attempts to "improve the breed." Indeed, Hofstadter's belief that eugenics is the "most enduring aspect of social Darwinism"[30] is supported by the enactment of sterilization laws in twenty states by shortly after World War I.[31] Paradoxically, though, eugenics also points to a crucial weakness of Spencer's theory. Social Darwinism insists that "conditions of existence" and "conditions of unfitness" are biogenic, and fails even to consider that these conditions might be socially constructed. That this thesis also exerted enduring consequences, is a point made in the discussion of eugenics and progressivism by Donald Pickens.[32] According to Pickens, while Spencer's beliefs stimulated eugenic philosophies, *negative* reactions to Spencer's theory spawned attempts at social reform. It is ironic that these "interventionist" efforts arose from a theory that argued for the necessity of *not* interfering with the natural progression of society. Whether Social Darwinism stimulated or justified eugenic practices may not be as central a question as it seems, for we have seen that parts of America's earlier "disability legislation" are almost certain social preconditions to eugenism.

Much of this legislation provided only for the maintenance of handicapped people. The general society alone did not bear its costs, for many handicapped people appear to have purchased the benefits of maintenance at the cost of their social equality. In colonial legislation, for example, provisions for the maintenance of handicapped citizens were accompanied by frank social exclusion. Although laws of the twentieth century offer handicapped people some degree of assimilation, they too seem characterized by the same kind of *quid pro quo* transactions.[33]

Hofstadter maintained that many economists of the period believed that their theories already expressed the concept of "survival of the fittest."[34] Of particular relevance to this chapter are the laissez-faire theories of the post-Civil War United States that declared a conceptual inconsistency between charity and a free society. For example, in *What Social Classes Owe to Each Other* (1883), William Graham Sumner argued that because the nation's social structure was based on contract, "one man . . . cannot claim help from, and cannot be charged to give help to, another."[35] Sumner's conclusion that charity (whether private or public) has no part in the American political structure, leads to questions about the quality of the citizenship of both the givers and takers of alms. A label of inferior citizenship probably had little impact on American philanthropists, for the giving of charity reflected a long legislative tradition that was usually a source of national pride. But the same legislative tradition often characterized the recipients of charity as objects of scorn, and Sumner's accusation may have added legitimacy to society's beliefs in their political inferiority.

In his discussion of the liberal social theories of the United States, Rimlinger[36] proposed that Social Darwinism had joined with American concepts of fundamentalist Protestantism to label recipients of charity as personal failures. As we have seen, however, the legislation of provincial Pennsylvania suggests a number of reasons for social disdain that are independent of the idea of personal failure. In almost every case, though, the behaviors informed by that disdain created a place on the margins of society for handicapped people. In contrast, Sumner's view of handicapped citizens as a clear menace to society's progress implied that they should occupy *no* social position:

> it may be said that those whom humanitarians and philanthropists call the weak are the ones through whom the productive and conservative forces of society are wasted. They constantly neutralize and destroy the finest efforts of the wise and the industrious, and are a deadweight on the society to realize any better things.[37]

Sumner's idea of the American political contract illuminates a major force in the construction of disability—beliefs that biological attributes determine social worth. Furthermore, his description of human ills illustrates one of the paradoxes inherent in America's social treatment of its handicapped population:

> Certain ills belong to the hardships of human life. They are natural. They are part of the struggle with Nature for existence, . . . and are to be met only by manly effort and energy. . . . Certain other ills are due to . . . the imperfections or errors of civil institutions. . . . [These] may be corrected by associated effort.[38]

Historically, the nation has usually rejected the notion of "natural ills," for handicapped people have often been the objects of one or another form of "associated effort." But by ignoring the possibility that civil institutions might themselves impose a sociopolitical handicap upon a physical handicap, America's legislation has created a category of ills that were *thought* to be natural.

Charity and Disability

As an American institution, charity was in large part a legislative creation. In order to understand the impact of that institution on the physically handicapped population, we will look at the disabling emphases of private charities, and at their incorporation into the Vocational Rehabilitation Act of 1920.

Most charitable agencies of the pre-Civil War period regarded poverty as a fixture of society, and approached its relief by attempting to fit their clients into the existing social structure. Because poverty was viewed in terms of personal virtue, attempts at its remediation often took the form of imposition of moral restraints.[39] Watson's history of the charitable movement reports that by the late 1800s, though, organized charities tried to deal with the impoverishing elements of society as well as with impoverished individuals.[40] By this time, recognition of social causes of poverty had stimulated many attempts at social and political reform. The broad range of efforts that comprised "the reform movement," however, did not appear to reflect ideas that disability is also a creation of the social structure.

Although many charitable agencies attempted to prevent disease and injury, people already physically infirm were apparently considered incapable of performing any social function except to receive society's good works. This view may have emerged from beliefs that such people could survive in no other manner. It is conceivable also that people had to be defined as dependent upon society in order to justify those good works (and workers). In any case, little or no attention was paid the possibility that acting *as if* the social abilities of handicapped people should be limited would actually impose limitations on personal independence and civil freedom.

By the early 1900s a number of agencies attempted to deal with physically handicapped men by teaching them the skills necessary for gainful employment. Sullivan and Snortum's presentation of these private vocational schools focused on their sponsorship, their basis of operation (for profit, or not), the vocational goals and expertness of the training they offered, and their connections to "parent" charities or hospitals.[41] The apparent concern of these writers was with how closely the schools were related to the normal society. This kind of classification also suggests that these agencies regarded disability as a biological "given" that can be relieved only by effecting change in physically impaired individuals.[42] In a sense, the focus of this typology anticipated Wolf Wolfensberger's concept of normalization.[43] As discussed in Chapter 1, Wolfensberger's method of helping mentally retarded people is to urge their conformity to the norms of appearance and behavior established by the general society.

Furthermore, because "rehabilitation" apparently was seen as a means to teach vocations rather than as a complex of methods to supply the array of social opportunities available to ablebodied people, the schools discussed by Sullivan and Snortum continued the assumption that physical limits constrict social and intellectual competence. Moreover, by defining handicapped people as charitable objects, charities legitimated their subjugation to the will of the (ablebodied) majority. One result of this definition was to force attention to the differences that distinguished these "objects" from ordinary poeple—a process that eventually resulted in inferences that turned physical defects into social defects. The following section shows how the practices of charities shaped results of the Vocational Rehabilitation Act of 1920.

The Vocational Rehabilitation Act of 1920

In April and May of 1918, the Joint Committee on Education conducted hearings on legislation intended to provide for the vocational rehabilitation of soldiers.[44] Although the bill was meant for members of the military, much of the testimony dealt with civilian rehabilitation. Since most of the presenters had administered voluntary rehabilitation agencies, they were able to offer both anecdotal and statistical evidence of the inadequacy of state care for handicapped civilians. They uniformly asserted that national legislation should also address the problem of civilians injured in industrial accidents. The testimony of R. M. Little, Director of the New York State Bureau for Vocational Rehabilitation, was typical:

> Our industries every year exact a frightful toll among the workingmen. Over 2,000,000 lost-time accidents occur every year; . . . . Every year there are more than 11,500 who suffer permanent functional disabilities in our industries. . . . I believe they are fundamentally entitled to the consideration of the National and State Governments in order that they also may have a chance to live out, as far as possible, a normal, independent, self-respecting life, and not be the victims of circumstances, left to shift for themselves, the objects of charity, to become mendicants and dependents upon public generosity.[45]

Little read into the record resolutions of the State Medical Association of California and of the State Conference of Social Agencies of California.[46] Each suggested that the bill be amended to provide rehabilitation for injured civilians. Moreover, each resolution implied that the idea of collective economic welfare that justified rehabilitation for injured workers also demanded rehabilitation for "victims of personal accidents." (After extensive debate in Congress, the law of 1920 included such "victims.")

One presenter spoke in terms of democratic theory when he described the proposed law as an instrument of civil equality:

> In considering [vocational rehabilitation], we must remember that the moral, social, and economic welfare of the individual is involved, and that the nation is only well served when everything has been done to sustain for the individual the very highest degree of citizenship.[47]

However, no congressman talked about this issue. As the debates discussed earlier suggested, a large segment of Congress intended the Vocational Rehabilitation Law of 1920 to protect the public economic welfare.

One of the last witnesses was Royal Meeker, Commissioner of Labor Statistics. Meeker began his testimony by submitting a letter he had written to President Wilson a month earlier in which he had urged a nationally initiated program of vocational rehabilitation to deal with the problem of industrial injuries. The letter clearly represented Meeker's view of the relative importance of these injuries:

> I am fully aware of the importance of taking care of war crip-
> ples, but, as important as this work is, it is insignificant com-
> pared to the vastly greater problem of providing for the
> rehabilitation and reemployment of industrial cripples.[48]

He then declared that the national mood of urgency along with the gen-erally accepted belief that America should sponsor rehabilitation for sol-diers would help to assure similar legislation for civilians. But Meeker found himself in a situation in which every other witness and every congressman on the committee proclaimed the necessity of military re-habilitation. The careful analysis that he had written gave way to seeming efforts to defend his patriotism:

> Of course the main thing is to get through the [military] reha-
> bilitation bill. I am for that first, last and all the time. That
> must be taken care of with the least possible delay. . . . I want to
> show what has happened to the industrial cripple, so that you
> men may bring the matter home to the Senate and to the House
> that if these things have happened to the industrial cripple, what
> may we expect to happen to the war cripple if nothing is done
> to rehabilitate him.[49]

Meeker's translation of the problem of civilian injuries into a reason for rehabilitating soldiers suggests that rehabilitation for civilians was con-ceptually, or at least legislatively, a distinct issue. Perhaps the Committee's perception of this distinction partly explains why it excluded the reha-bilitation of civilians from the proposed law for soldiers.

Despite this decision, however, Representative William Bankhead and Senator Hoke Smith introduced bills for the promotion of civilian voca-tional rehabilitation.[50] Although the bills were never considered by the whole Congress, their introduction may have been meant to assure the people concerned with handicapped civilians that their interests were not forgotten, and that the military vocational rehabilitation bill was simply a "detour" necessitated by the war.

As did the Military Rehabilitation Act, the Bankhead/Smith bills wel-comed charitable gifts:

> That the Federal Board for Vocational Education is hereby au-
> thorized and empowered to receive such gifts and donations

from either public or private sources as may be offered uncondi-
tionally. All moneys received . . . shall constitute a permanent
fund to be called the "Special fund for the vocational rehabilitation of disabled persons"—to be administered by the Federal
Board.[51]

The provision indicates that handicapped individuals were still characterized as objects of private charity whose position in society was to be
defined by others. Identical language in the Vocational Rehabilitation Act
of 1920 permits an identical inference. By 1973, however, rehabilitation
legislation no longer asked for the gifts of philanthropists. Nevertheless it
did continue the long-standing connection between handicap and charity
by soliciting the unpaid time and advice of citizens concerned with the
welfare of physically impaired people.[52]

The nation's use of private charity has clearly changed in form through
the centuries since the Duke's Laws. However, what seems to be a denial
of public responsibility remains. Little's wish to make the handicapped
population independent of "public generosity" clearly was not fulfilled by
these pieces of rehabilitation legislation.

Chapter 2 examined the enactment of the Act of 1920 in relation to
the legislation for vocational education and military rehabilitation that
had preceded it. That context suggested a particular set of explanations
for its effects. In this chapter, looking at that same Vocational Rehabilitation Act of 1920 in relation to earlier treatment of handicapped civilians
advances additional explanations:

1. This federal law may have served fewer vocational rehabilitants than
was possible because it was structured to comply with the tradition of
individual state responsibility for "unfortunates."

2. Segregated training emerged from institutionalized assumptions that
physical difference *requires* a marginal social position.

3. The law's implicit link between people's value and their ability to
work permitted assimilation for a few while decreasing possible social
absorption for millions of others.

Because each of these three explanations represents elements of the construct of disability, it is important to elaborate on them.

The Tradition of State Care

Historically, providing for the care of handicapped civilians was the
responsibility of individual states. But when lawmakers became aware that

private rehabilitation agencies were able to train some injured people to support themselves, Congress responded by proposing federal involvement in programs of vocational rehabilitation. These national arrangements, however, were to provide only for the *promotion* of rehabilitation. Although simply allowing rehabilitation may have represented a necessary political strategy, failing to demand such programs may have resulted in fewer handicapped people being served by the Act. Although this suggestion is not empirically testable, it does seem likely that the numbers of possible rehabilitants would have differed if the federal government had compelled, rather than permitted, the development of this program.

Sullivan and Snortum described the limited national involvement in civilian vocational rehabilitation:

> The rehabilitation of civilians is a state matter. It is dependent upon state initiative. The participation of the Federal government in it extends only to granting financial aid and to providing an advisory service.[53]

No state was forced to accept this national law, nor was it forced to develop any scheme for rehabilitating its handicapped citizens. Each state was to receive federal advice and funds only if it chose to adopt a plan acceptable to the Federal Board for Vocational Rehabilitation. Many states did accept the Law's provisions (by 1921, thirty-five states;[54] by 1932, forty-four states),[55] but each established its own criteria for the eligibility of rehabilitants. This obvious diversity of standards, as well as variations in the competency of evaluators, probably led to differences in the numbers of accepted trainees.

Problems of financial support of rehabilitants also can be traced to the tradition of state care. State workmen's compensation laws were already in place, and the national Vocational Rehabilitation Act required the cooperation of the related state agencies.[56] But a substantial number of rehabilitants had been injured in non-compensable accidents or had become physically handicapped via disease or congenital disorder. Whether these people were to be maintained while undertaking rehabilitation training, and if so, how, were decisions left to each state. Pennsylvania approached this problem by developing a special "maintenance fund" to be administered at the discretion of its Board for Rehabilitation.[57] According to Sullivan and Snortum, however, many states declined to establish a specific fund, and used instead their existing systems of public relief.[58] Several states made the connection between rehabilitation and charity even stronger by depending on the good will of philanthropists.[59] According to the statute of 1920, the federal government allocated funds for the establishment of vocational rehabilitation programs in proportion to state populations.[60] Because the economic problem posed by physical handicap was considered a national problem, it is difficult to understand why funds for the maintenance of people who had "caused" the problem were not allocated in that way as well.

Segregated Trainees

Handicapped vocational trainees usually were segregated. One reason for such practices may have been the assumption that handicapped persons *should* be segregated. An example of such an assumption can be found in John Culbert Faries' analysis of several years of work with handicapped men:

> [I]t is often discouraging for a handicapped worker to initiate his training alongside a normal person, but where he works with other handicapped persons his pride will lead him to minimize his disability and strive to excel in his work.[61]

The psychological mechanisms that Faries implies may exist, but his anecdotal observations neither support his bold assertions, nor allow for evaluation of the suggested mechanisms.[62]

The somewhat similar assumption that training with other handicapped adults bolsters confidence and therefore facilitates adaptation, may be another source of segregation. In their discussion of the conditions that promote effective vocational rehabilitation, Sullivan and Snortum state that such a training condition is desirable. But they also indicate that segregation is not entirely meritorious:

> A selected student body as compared with a very general and unselected one in few if any respects is more desirable for rehabilitation wards. It is true these persons need contact with the masses. They are of them and belong to them. But the very fact that they are more mature means that the adjustment to a group will be more easily made with the private school group.[63]

Their untested premise may also reflect a belief that segregation is a naturally congenial condition for handicapped people.

Although both citations refer to vocational training, a presumption of the desirability of segregation can also be seen in other forms of education.

This assumption, for example, has often been invoked to justify resistance to "mainstreaming" handicapped school children. Sullivan and Snortum's implication that integration favors the social adaptation of handicapped children was ignored for many years, perhaps because those children were not expected to become part of the general society.

While each state was to rule on the qualifications of potential clients, the federal government, in a statement of policy written by Dr. Little, insisted that methods of casework were to be used in the process of their rehabilitation:

> The rehabilitation service is not group work, nor can it be suc-
> cessfully accomplished by the usual standards of school work.
> Physically handicapped persons do not fit well into standards for
> normal pupils. Experience shows that the rehabilitation of the
> disabled is a highly complex, specialized personal service, which
> must take form according to the peculiar difficulties and apti-
> tude of each person. . . . Every physically handicapped person
> presents a number of distinct problems which the rehabilitation
> workers must deal with sympathetically and with imagination,
> patience, and ingenuity. Case-work methods, therefore, are fun-
> damental to success in rehabilitation.[64]

Possibly because of their emphasis on individual differences, casework methods may have promoted a kind of deviance analysis that sought causes of abnormality within *persons* rather than within society's norms. Incorporating these methods into official policy may then have helped to legitimize practices of segregation.

Measurement of Value by Work

The Vocational Rehabilitation Act of 1920 has been evaluated elsewhere in terms of the numbers of handicapped people served, the proportion of handicapped people placed in competitive employment, and the availability and nature of teaching and placement services.[65] Such exact measures are clearly useful to understanding results of this law. But the Act's implicit judgments of the value of some handicapped people may also have had an important effect, for the contrast suggested by such appraisals could have decreased the valuation of other handicapped people, and therefore de-creased the likelihood of their integration.

What seem to be instances of this relative devaluation occurred in later decades. When President Franklin Roosevelt combined federal activities concerned with welfare and health into a single agency,[66] his attempt to increase efficiency probably permitted a larger number of handicapped people to join the workforce. The number of people that could be gainfully employed was probably also boosted when new medical and surgical techniques of physical restoration were incorporated into national law, a process described in Berkowitz's *Federal Response to Disability.*[67] But by increasing the visibility of this favored class of handicapped citizens, each of these administrative and legislative strategies may have sanctioned the negative attitudes of society toward those incapable of work, making integration of this "subgroup" even less likely.

Furthermore, even though handicapped people worked, they were denied the extra-vocational intercourse available to ablebodied people. Some part of this denial was probably a matter of architectural inaccessibility. However, considering available construction techniques, many architectural barriers were, and are, unnecessary. Such barriers may certainly reflect thoughtlessness and indifference, but their existence may also express beliefs that people who are physically handicapped do not belong in the mainstream of society. Neither the Act of 1920, nor the private vocational rehabilitation agencies that had preceded it, indicated that vocational assimilation was meant as a stage toward the desired end of social integration—although possibly some theorists believed that the mechanism of "contact" would eventually produce full social integration. Vocational assimilation may have been seen as the only path toward civil equality that should be made available to handicapped people.

Notes

1. Gordon S. Watkins, *An Introduction to the Study of Labor Problems,* p. 213.

2. Staughton George, Benjamin N. Nead and Thomas McCamant, eds., *Charter to William Penn. . . . The Duke's Laws . . . .*, p. 47.

3. Province of Pennsylvania, *An Act for Amending the Laws Relating to the Poor,* Sect. II. (1748–49), Vol. V, p. 79.

4. George et al., *Charter to William Penn . . . The Duke's Laws,* p. 58.

5. Ibid., p. 18.

6. William Clinton Heffner, *History of Poor Relief Legislation in Pennsylvania, 1682–1913.*

7. Ibid., pp. 273–87.

8. Province of Pennsylvania, *An Act For the Better Provision for the Poor Within This Province and Territories.* (1700), Vol. II, p. 20.

9. Province of Pennsylvania, *An Act for Amending the Laws Relating to the Poor,* Sect. IX. (1748–49), Vol. V, p. 85.

10. U.S., *An Act to provide for vocational rehabilitation and return to civil employment of disabled persons discharged from the military . . . .* (1918); *An Act to provide for the promotion of vocational rehabilitation of persons disabled in industry or otherwise and their return to civil employment.* (1920).

11. Province of Pennsylvania, *An Act for the Relief of the Poor*, Sect. V. (1705–06), Vol. II, p. 253.

12. Province of Pennsylvania, *An Act for Supplying some Defects in the Law for the Relief of the Poor*, Sect. II. (1718), Vol. III, p. 224.

13. Ibid., Preface. (1718), Vol. III, p. 221.

14. Province of Pennsylvania, *An Act Imposing a Duty on Persons Convicted of Heinous Crimes Brought Into this Province and Not Warranted by the Laws of Great Britain, and to Prevent Poor and Impotent Persons Being Imported into the Same*, Sect. IX. (1743–43), Vol. IV, p. 368.

15. Province of Pennsylvania, *An Act Laying a Duty on Foreigners and Irish Servants Imported into this Province*, Preface (1729), Vol. IV, p. 135.

16. Province of Pennsylvania, *An Act Imposing a Duty on Persons Convicted of Heinous Crimes and to Prevent Poor and Impotent Persons Being Imported into the Province of Pennsylvania*, Sect. I. (1729–30), Vol. IV, p. 164.

17. Ibid., Sect. III, p. 167.

18. George et al., *Charter to William Penn . . . the Duke's Laws*, pp. 38–39.

19. Richard Hofstadter, *Social Darwinism in American Thought*, pp. 5, 31–32.

20. Herbert Spencer, *Social Statics; or The Conditions Essential to Human Happiness*.

21. Ibid., p. 79.

22. Ibid., p. 356.

23. Ibid., p. 349.

24. Ibid., p. 357.

25. Ibid., Preface.

26. Ibid., Ch. XXI, "The Duty of the State," pp. 276–301; Ch. XXII, "The Limit of State-Duty," pp. 301–25.

27. William Bateson, "Biological Fact and the Structure of Society," pp. 24–25.

28. Spencer, *Social Statics*, p. 355.

29. Seymour Sarason and John Doris, *Psychological Problems in Mental Deficiency;* see esp. chapters 11–17, and see pp. 271–73 for reference to Bateson.

30. Hofstadter, *Social Darwinism*, p. 161.

31. Ibid., pp. 102–30.

32. Donald K. Pickens, *Eugenics and the Progressives*, p. 91.

33. Neil Gilbert and Harry Specht's *Dimensions of Social Work Policy* analyzes general welfare policies in these terms.

34. Hofstadter, *Social Darwinism*, pp. 143–47.

35. William Graham Sumner, *What Social Classes Owe To Each Other*, p. 27.

36. Gaston V. Rimlinger, *Welfare Policy and Industrialization in Europe, America and Russia*, pp. 46–51.

37. Sumner, *Social Classes*, pp. 20–21.

38. Ibid., pp. 17–18.

39. Frank D. Watson, *The Charity Organization Movement in the United States*, pp. 66–69.

40. Ibid., pp. 275–80.

41. Oscar M. Sullivan and Kenneth O. Snortum, *Disabled Persons: Their Education and Rehabilitation*, pp. 225–39.

42. An apparent analogy to the early conception of poverty.

43. Wolf Wolfensberger, *The Principle of Normalization in Human Services*.

44. U.S. Congressional Joint Committee on Education, *Hearings* on H.R. 11367 and S. 4284, bills for military vocational rehabilitation. (65-2).

45. Ibid., Statement of R. M. Little, p. 82.

46. Ibid., pp. 85–88.

47. Ibid., Statement of Allen Walker, p. 9.

48. Ibid., Statement of Royal Meeker, p. 108.

49. Ibid., p. 110. The change in Meeker's emphasis indicates how the process of lawmaking can respond to the influence of a small group.

50. Sen. Hoke Smith introduced S. 4922 (65-3) on Dec. 26, 1918; Rep. William Bankhead introduced H.R. 12880 (65-3) on Feb. 13, 1919.

51. H.R. 12880, Sect. V.

52. U.S., *An Act to extend the Rehabilitation Act of 1973* . . . . (1974), p. 367.

53. Sullivan and Snortum, *Disabled Persons,* p. 164.

54. Federal Board for Vocational Education, *Fifth Annual Report to Congress,* p. 25.

55. Federal Board for Vocational Education, *16th Annual Report to Congress,* p. 59.

56. U.S., *An Act to provide for vocational rehabilitation of persons disabled in industry . . . ,* Sect. 3 (1920).

57. S. S. Riddle, "Rehabilitating the Worker When Accident Prevention Fails," p. 223.

58. Sullivan and Snortum, *Disabled Persons,* pp. 317–18.

59. Ibid., p. 320.

60. U.S., *An Act to provide for vocational rehabilitation of persons disabled in industry,* Sect. 1 (1920). This first law that provided for rehabilitation of civilians allocated funds proportionate to each state's population. The formulas of subsequent federal rehabilitation laws were weighted by per capita income.

61. John Culbert Faries, *Three Years of Work for Handicapped Men: A Report of the Activities of the Institute for Crippled and Disabled Men,* p. 27.

62. To some degree, Faries' conclusions anticipate those tenets of Social Comparison Theory that enable prediction of physical performance. However, of the many empirical studies that support this theory, I know of none that focuses on the physical performance of *handicapped adults.*

63. Sullivan and Snortum, *Disabled Persons,* p. 229.

64. R. M. Little, "Economic and Social Significance of the Vocational Rehabilitation Program," pp. 9–10.

65. E.g., Riddle's "Rehabilitating the Worker" discusses such assessments in the Commonwealth of Pennsylvania.

66. U.S. *Reorganization Plan No. 1,* Part 2. *Federal Security Agency.* Prepared by the President and transmitted to Congress (76-1) pursuant to the provisions of the Reorganization Act of 1939.

67. Edward David Berkowitz, *Rehabilitation: The Federal Government's Response to Disability, 1935–1954.*

CHAPTER 5

Disability and Education: Physically Handicapped Children

He, whose Mind directs not wisely, will never take the right Way; and he, whose Body is crazy and feeble, will never be able to advance in it.

John Locke, *Some Thoughts Concerning Education.*[1]

The thesis central to this book is that early public policies have created a disabling atmosphere that helps to translate physical defects into social defects. This chapter further illustrates that argument by showing that the truthfulness of Locke's prophecy frequently depends not on physical inabilities but on inferences promoted by American education. Historical analysis suggests that educational institutions create this effect by transmitting beliefs that individuals with physical impairments belong to a category called "the handicapped." This labeling process and its consequences in turn indicate that stereotypy and segregated education have become so interrelated that one set of practices both justifies and generates the other. To the extent that this sequence causes the dysfunction of physically impaired people, it is a major source of disability.

The first section of the chapter focuses on public education from the colonial era to the first half of the nineteenth century. Records of the early years of this period do not indicate the existence of handicapped children in public schools.[2] While such records might of course mean that the statistics of the time did not specify the physical condition of students, they may also indicate that some handicapped children failed to survive until of school age. The case of Philadelphia shows how this latter alternative may have operated. Education in that city was as accessible to children as any place in colonial America, with the exception of some Massachusetts towns. Philadelphia's archives,[3] however, offer no indication that handicapped children were among them. The count by the United States Census of 1790[4] of 5,270 "free white males under 16 years" indicates that approximately 10,000 children lived in the city. The inability to prevent or combat infections suggests that many children with physical infirmities would not have survived for more than days or weeks. If the incidence rates of major physical abnormalities—congenital or acquired by disease or accident—were similar to those of today, few handicapped children existed.

This medical likelihood, however, does not tell the whole story either. A third determinant is possible: America's prevailing view of education as an instrument for realizing a child's economic potential resulted in handicapped children having been excluded from school. A variation on this possible cause can be seen in Pennsylvania's Constitutional Convention of 1837. The debates of this convention suggest that defining education as an economic tool encouraged the general society to believe that physically impaired people are necessarily marked by the attributes of moral deficiency and civic incompetence. Another related cause of the failure to provide for educating handicapped children, may have been the view that the dependence of these children was an immutable physical fact. Although each of these beliefs has been alluded to earlier, this chapter will look at them further by showing their relationship to institutionalized segregation.

Several portions of these same debates suggest that another aspect of disability derives from the political process of dealing with a minority group. This possibility also was introduced earlier when it was suggested that an address by Theodore Roosevelt had shown that majoritarian processes can impose political impotence on a statistically small segment of the population. However, the treatment of handicapped people as a political minority suggests another cause for their marginal status: attributions of inferiority are stimulated by a quiet, passive, acceptance of a subordinate social position. This process of "self-infliction" seems analytically distinct from the often-discussed process in which society's accepted views teach handicapped people to identify themselves as inferior.

The second part of the chapter centers on the debates concerning education in the proceedings of Pennsylvania's Constitutional Convention of 1873. These debates permit the argument that delegating the education of handicapped children to private organizations both prompted their separation from ablebodied children, and advanced a view that these children did not need—or perhaps merit—publicly initiated education. It seems likely, therefore, that the later practice of endorsing and incorporating the educational schemes of private charities taught physically abnormal children to think of themselves in terms of "worth." Moreover, while government's institutionalization of the position of the beneficiary may well account for one component of "the handicapped" label, the debates of 1873 show once again that the attributes of threat and perpetual childhood also contributed to this label.

The chapter ends by examining education in the late nineteenth and early twentieth centuries. During this period a number of states initiated the education of handicapped children and no longer simply supported the educational arrangements of existing private institutions. It has been argued elsewhere that this change in government action represented a new commitment to democratic equality.[5] But as will become clear, these publicly sponsored efforts continued to permit differential civil privileges and obligations.

The chapter as a whole provides additional support to the argument that the evaluation of disability legislation requires an understanding of its historical development. For example, several recent articles on "mainstreaming"[6] ask whether the 1975 law mandating public education for all handicapped children[7] can achieve the integration apparently intended by the clause "least restrictive environment." The writers generally attribute failures in integration to the problem of resolving competing claims on perceptively scarce national resources. As this book has argued, judgments about scarcity of public resources can be affected by the deeply embedded tradition of devaluating handicapped people. In this chapter that traditional process of devaluating will be looked at as a source of segregation.

Colonial and Early National Education

Although the structure and availability of schooling in the colonies varied considerably, instructional content seems to have been fairly uniform. Descriptions in almost every history of American education[8] indicate that public documents proclaimed education as the transmitter of democratic values. Apparently, however, many Americans really expected public education to assure the support of the nation's future families. For although most children were taught to read to the extent that they might know the laws of the colony, only boys were taught to write and to cypher—important skills for the practice of a trade.

The education provision of Pennsylvania's Constitution of 1790 exemplifies this expectation. Although one might interpret this portion of the document as a noble conveyor of democratic values or as a strategy advanced to prevent political rebellion, it may actually have been intended to protect the Commonwealth from the burden of economically dependent people: "The legislature shall, as soon as conveniently may be, provide, by law, for the establishment of schools throughout the State, in such manner that the poor may be taught gratis."[9]

Pennsylvania's 1837 Constitutional Convention also appeared to address the question of how to sustain society's economic well-being. The delegates to the convention gave much consideration to providing instruction "in the English or German language, as may be by law directed,"[10] apparently hoping that children's knowledge of the language of the state would be of both political and economic benefit. The debates over the language of instruction are fascinating, for they anticipate many of the recent arguments that concern bilingual education. However, the passage cited below suggests that the discussion of conserving public resources was partially reflective of society's devaluation of handicapped people. Arguing that the availability of teaching in their native tongue would make Pennsylvania especially appealing to German immigrants, Ingersoll stated that: "[E]ven if paupers come, they will render us great service, if they come with arms, hands and legs and are able to work."[11]

Two groups of evidence suggest that some of Ingersoll's concern for Pennsylvania's solvency reflected scorn of people without "arms, hands and legs." As discussed earlier, one set of data is embodied in the precepts of religious orthodoxy. Although the Constitution of 1790 did not limit public education to children of poor families, most towns paid only for the education of indigent youth (a term apparently applied to mulatto, Indian, and illegitimate children, as well as to the children of paupers). Presumably in response to the large number of students made undesirable by religious correlations between poverty and personal fault, many private schools with diverse academic and vocational curricula appeared. Perhaps the size of the population that experienced poverty was too great to accept such negative characterization for long. In a similar but contrary fashion, perhaps society accepted doctrines relating a child's virtue to his potential for usefulness because only a few people had personal reason to reject them.

The potency of this proclaimed connection between poverty and fault can be seen in the kinds of questions raised centuries later. For example, Dr. Gwilym Davis's 1914 analysis of the education of handicapped children appears to assume that character defects exist disproportionately among them:

> While intellectual development is of importance it is insignificant as compared with good character. . . . The problem is how to

rear them [cripples] so that they shall develop into industrious, unselfish, honest and reliable citizens. How can they ever be made to be self-supporting if they are lazy and unwilling to work? How can ambition be infused into them so that they will endeavor to help themselves instead of being content to be parasites on the body politic?[12]

The second kind of evidence that suggests disdain in Ingersoll's words is represented in Robert Coram's 1791 proposal for a system of public education. Although he did not refer at all to physical dependence, Coram interpreted the attribute of dependency as a liability to the community:

To conclude, to make men happy, the first step is to make them independent. For if they are dependent, they can neither manage their private concerns properly, retain their own dignity, or vote impartially for their country: they can be but tools at best.[13]

A delegate to the 1837 convention appears to build on Coran's view of dependence with an address that seems to convert physical soundness into a sign of Americanism:

No man is poor in this country, who is able to work, as there is work for all; and this work is a capital which all have, who have health and strength.[14]

The assumptions of civil inadequacy and the implicit connection between an able body and patriotism probably both justified and fostered beliefs that physically handicapped people should be kept out of the mainstream of society. The following example shows that an absence of Constitutional recognition may have helped to transform these beliefs into practice.

Talking of German-speaking children, Mr. Merrill stated in a session of the 1837 convention: "Give them a chance to obtain some intelligence in their own language, and then they will be more able to see the necessity of coming into the language of the state."[15] Several delegates told of instances, though, in which local mandates legislating instruction in German were ignored. They concluded that such ordinances would be enforceable only with the support of a specific constitutional imperative.[16] While addressing the general problem of compliance with law is certainly beyond the purpose of this book, it should be noted that the need for a constitutional directive to assure the assimilation of an ethnic minority may also exist with the handicapped segment of the population.

The proposal to teach in German points to another aspect of the stereotype that education has helped to create. German-speaking children were classified as "special" only as long as they did not know the language of the state. Once they learned English they were accepted as members of the majority. With physically handicapped children, however, public education perpetuated beliefs that such children are, and always will be, special. The problem with the attribution of specialness to handicapped people, of course, is its creation of disability. Most theories of personality development suggest that the classmates of children designated as special will retain these attributions even into adulthood. This book does not deal with the psychological problems that may arise when physically handicapped people learn to view themselves as special, even though feelings of "entitlement" certainly may be one source of disablement. But if handicapped people are viewed as special throughout their lifetimes, how can either their own will, or society's efforts to compensate for their physical defects, lead to their treatment as ordinary citizens?

A proposal that might have eliminated the legal basis of their specialness was introduced in Pennsylvania's 1837 convention. The Committee on Education unanimously reported this amendment:

> The legislature shall, as soon as conveniently may be, provide, by law, for the establishment of schools throughout the state, in such manner that *all* children be taught at public expense. [my emphasis][17]

Several delegates disapproved of the phrase "[T]he legislature shall, as soon as conveniently may be." Mr. Read, for example, insisted that such language implied dissatisfaction with the effectiveness of forty-five years of legislative efforts. Apparently proud of the developing system of education, or unwilling to offend individual legislators, he suggested instead "shall continue to provide."[18] However, most delegates seemed to fear that any change of language would "prejudice, instead of promoting, the cause of education."[19] For example:

> The system is now rapidly gaining ground, and if we act wisely and carefully, it will still continue to gain ground; but if we insert in the constitution some obligatory clause, you will cause the people to rise up against it, and we will lose all at one blow that we have gained in years.[20]

The pre-Civil War populist urges that apparently accounted for altered practices of banks and corporations did not extend to this part of the

Constitutional Article on Education. The section was not changed. Perhaps rejecting the phrase "all children" was a by-product of a plan intended to assure educational progress. But its rejection, and the retention of the language of 1790, also may have reflected the idea that children with physical impairments simply *were not* the proper concern of public education.

Paradoxically, the failure of this element of populism indicates that the democratic process of formulating educational policy may itself be a source of the label "the handicapped." The principle of respecting the wishes of the majority in this case means following the desires of parents of ablebodied children. Practicing the majoritarian principle thus seems to deny the traditional belief that

> [T]he greater the extent of the education which you can give,
> the better will it be for the liberties of the country, and the more
> sure will be the prospect that those dear and sacred liberties
> will be transmitted unimpaired to our children.[21]

The apparent exclusion of handicapped children from public education also suggests beliefs that these children did not need those "dear and sacred liberties," or perhaps, that such a need was ignored.

Considering this decision from the perspective developed by Gordon Wood's *Creation of the American Republic*[22] raises the possibility that educational interests of minorities *per se* are not of public concern. In Wood's interpretation, early republicans conceived of American politics as an institution meant to transcend private interests and to encourage actions beneficial to a public whole. He offers a number of excerpts from sermons and from essays of Whig activists to support his view that

> [T]he sacrifice of individual interests to the greater good of the
> whole formed the essence of republicanism and comprehended
> for Americans the idealistic goal of their Revolution. . . . This re-
> publican ideology both presumed and helped shape the Ameri-
> cans' conception of the way their society and politics should be
> structured and operated. . . . By 1776 the Revolution came to
> represent a final attempt . . . by many Americans to realize the
> traditional Commonwealth ideal of a corporate society, in which
> the common good would be the only objective of government.[23]

Wood then proceeds to demonstrate that instead of aiming to achieve "the comon good," the primary function of American political institutions soon became that of reconciling the interests of individuals.[24] This conception of politics (one with very broad explanatory power) suggests that categorizing handicapped people as members of a political minority diminishes the likelihood that their interests will be served. Indeed, when compulsory education was considered in 1873, physically handicapped children were effectively excluded: "They [the legislators] may by law require that every child of sufficient mental and physical ability shall attend the public schools, unless educated by other means."[25] The motivating force of the "traditional commonwealth ideal" suggests that the standard of "sufficient mental and physical ability" was meant to exclude with *the legitimacy of law* those children thought of as economically useless to society. The pressures of conflicting private interests implicit in Wood's representation indicate that such an explanation attends to both the quantitative smallness and the political impotence of this population segment.

This section will conclude by relating this syndrome of economic productivity and societal usefulness to America's emphasis on efficiency. The Frame of Government that William Penn established for Pennsylvania in 1776 stated:

> A school or schools shall be established in each county by the legislature, for the convenient instruction of youth, with such salaries to the masters paid by the public, as may enable them to instruct youth at low prices.[26]

Pennsylvania's Constitution of 1873 also seemed to express this concern for "cost effectiveness":

> The General Assembly shall provide for the maintenance and support of a thorough and efficient system of public schools, wherein all the children of this commonwealth above the age of six years may be educated, and shall appropriate at least one million dollars each year for that purpose.[27]

The positive value that Americans attached to efficiency has also been seen in the earlier discussion of workmen's compensation legislation. In this chapter the emphasis put on economic productivity by educational institutions suggests a similar assessment. Indeed, it seems reasonable to infer that the valuation of efficiency was one factor that precluded thinking of handicapped children as part of "all children above the age of six years."

The following section continues to explore the disabling process by showing that the practices of segregating and discrediting handicapped children are in large part products of organized charities.

Charity and the Education of Children with Handicaps

An 1827 Philadelphia Town Meeting defined the claims of physically impotent citizens as political rights:

> That the virtuous poor, in a state of superannuation or sickness, or infirmity disabling them from earning a subsistence, have a rightful claim on society for a decent and even a comfortable subsistence.[28]

Although the fragment refers to adults, the possession of civil rights is, of course, part of the potentiality of childhood. But rather than expressing this pure contractual obligation—a relationship proper to citizens *qua* citizens—public education of handicapped children often has reflected discretion and kindness. This distorted conception of political obligation—one that diminishes people with benevolence—is a major disabling consequence of designating private charities as official agencies.

By the second half of the nineteenth century, towns and counties began to assist institutions for handicapped children. The nature of community aid varied—some towns sent teachers from public schools to instruct handicapped children, some towns allocated public funds to private schools.[29] In 1869, the legislature of Pennsylvania decided that aiding schools for handicapped children, along with prisons and alms houses, was a government responsibility. A Board of Public Charities[30] was formed to implement the state's decision; its annual report of 1871 stated that "charities that rescue children from lives of depredation, serve the State by saving its public wealth."[31] As did several of the public documents cited earlier, this report indicated that government's concern for handicapped children expressed as much responsibility for the economic welfare of the state as for the lives of individual citizens.

A Philadelphia delegate to Pennsylvania's Constitutional Convention of 1873 seems to have expressed a similar bias when he spoke about the private charities within the Commonwealth that cared for "our insane and our deaf and dumb."[32] He first defined the value of these institutions in terms of the broad population that might use them:

> Our insane and our deaf and dumb from all parts of the State are admitted to the benefits afforded by these institutions in the cities. It is not alone the locality in which these institutions happen to be that is interested in them.[33]

Then, after proclaiming that aid to these charities is "a noble and christian" [*sic*] endeavor, he declared that such charities should be made into agents of the state. However, his speech indicated that direct care for these citizens was not part of his conception of public obligation:

> Is there any more noble use to which we can devote a small portion of our public funds than to the aid of these charities to assist in taking care of those . . . who we must take care of as amply as it is possible for us to do?[34]

Further evidence that educating handicapped children represented an abdication of government responsibility can be inferred from a book written more than fifty years later. In that book, *The Crippled and the Disabled* (1935), the prominent physician Henry Kessler wrote that the education of handicapped children reflected "a gradual transfer from private to public responsibility."[35] Many of Kessler's examples support his assertion, but when one measures public responsibility by existing opportunities for personal actualization, the "gradual transfer" in America can be seen to have been only partial. Considered in the context of the debates of 1873, Kessler's review suggests that whether educating handicapped children was thought of as a cost effective maneuver or as a practice compliant with Christian precepts, it was in great part a political problem.

Another delegate to the 1873 convention pointed to the public interests served by the functions of private schools and asylums:

> [t]his Commonwealth has as great a necessity in providing for the charitable objects which exist within its bounds as it has in the education of its youth. It has a great necessity in restoring sanity to the insane, and strength to those who are decrepit and broken down in life, and in all the other forms of public charity it has as great a necessity in restoring them to usefulness in the community as it has in education and bringing up its youth to be useful and beneficial citizens of the State. . . . on that ground I submit that this matter of public charity is a matter of public concern, and should be favored and promoted just as much as we would favor and promote the cause of public education.[36]

While the phrase "public charity" might have been intended to describe a method meant to assure civil usefulness, it probably also promoted segregated public education. Furthermore, this language clearly distinguished the state's care of "charitable objects" from "the education of its youth." To the extent that this distinction expressed a widely held view, it points to a set of attitudes that helped to transform handicapped children into disabled adults.

Another method of connecting charity to the state can be seen in efforts to regulate private charities:

> I believe . . . in giving to some—only a few of these charities. . . . There ought to be some restriction—some discrimination. I do not believe the Legislature has a right to tax the people heavily and then give away the money they extorted, without just discrimination.[37]

Unlike those who favored regulatory schemes, however, several delegates advanced the position that charity simply is not a public function. For example,

> I have become fully satisfied that the whole system of donating or giving away public money to charity is radically wrong. I am opposed, not only to all union between the church and the State, but also between the State and private charities. I maintain, as a principle, that no legislative body . . . has the right to give away the public moneys raised by taxation . . . to any charitable purpose whatever. . . . I submit that private charities should depend upon the sympathy and the generosity of private individuals.[38]

But the attempted prevention of publicly sponsored charities failed. The delegates to the convention decided that the usefulness of charities to the state justified their public support. Thus the link between charity and the civil status of physically handicapped people became increasingly firm.

In an earlier chapter it was proposed that organized charities impose disability by using methods that exaggerate the dependency of their physically impaired clients. We have seen in this chapter that the government decision to support charities has specified two additional causes of disability. First, as was suggested earlier, permitting organized charities to educate handicapped children can be interpreted as a denial of a civil right. Second, public incorporation of the concept of charity may have stimulated the construction of separate systems of public education. The 1870 report of the nation's Commissioner of Education gives credence to this second proposition:

> The schools for the deaf, dumb, and blind are fast passing out of the class known as charitable, and becoming part and parcel

of the system of public education. It is hoped that ere long every State will have made ample provision for the establishment and conduct of these schools.[39]

According to Kessler's *The Crippled and the Disabled,* the first state institution for cripples was established in Nebraska in 1899.[40] (Kessler notes that Pennsylvania did not initiate state care until 1923.)[41] What had once been purely custodial institutions for orthopedically impaired children often became schools linked to public hospitals and dispensaries. Special schools, usually copied from Western European institutions, were developed for blind, deaf and feeble-minded children.[42] But, as the discussion below indicates, forces other than the power of a model have effected disability, and several other disabling consequences have grown out of the institution of public education.

In the 1873 debates Mr. Wherry proposed compulsory industrial schools for "vagrant, neglected and abandoned children."[43] He supported his proposal by citing a study[44] that identified vagrant and abandoned children as a major source of crime. Wherry saw these children as "*doomed* to live lives of want and crime and woe *through ignorance.*"[45] Along with many other delegates he concluded that educating these children would protect the general population of Pennsylvania. But conceiving of education as an instrument of police power probably helped to reinforce the element of threat in the image held of handicapped children. Furthermore, such a view suggests an interrelationship between segregation and notions that handicapped children are a menace to society.

Wherry's proposal was eventually rejected as violating the natural rights of parents. Specifically, Mr. Purman declared that the likelihood of errors in judging which children are "neglected" and "neglected in what" comprised an unacceptable risk to the sanctity of "the power of parents over their children."[46] That the beginnings of state involvement in the education of incurably handicapped children represented a similar form of power is suggested by a statement made years later by the superintendent of the Cleveland public schools: "Our aim is to make these children feel that they are doing what children ordinarily do, and living the natural life."[47] The issue of parental rights and the practice of transferring rights— and obligations—to an institution caring for children, raises many questions. But because handicapped adults are often as dependent as children, an unquestioned societal assumption of parental rights may occur. Furthermore, since segregating handicapped people assures knowledge of their whereabouts, the parent/child relationship[48] may have been one source of practices of segregation. A substantial part of the marginality of physically handicapped adults may thus be caused by the institution-alization of this asymmetrical relationship.

Another objection to Wherry's proposal suggests that social distinctions *create* differences. Moreover, its language appears to contain the notion that "separate is not equal":

> I assert that the true way to reform and bring up into proper manhood these children now neglected is to bring them into the common schools of the State and not to build houses here and there about Philadelphia and other cities written upon them "for neglected and abandoned children"; *for that very thing will make them abandoned.* . . . You cannot take the favored children of a ward in Philadelphia and put them into one school and the poor and unfortunate into another school and give them the advantages that the system of education is intended to accomplish. . . . Let us have no distinctions, no separate provisions for one class of children over another; provide for them all in the same section and all alike. [my emphasis][49]

The subsequent formation of separate schools indicates that the reasoning of this assertion did not prevail. However, this acknowledgment of the "self-fulfilling" nature of the process of categorizing suggests that beliefs of childhood translate into actions of adults.

Possibly, Pennsylvania's nineteenth-century constitutional debates concerning *higher* education also contributed to the construct of disability. The state's 1776 Constitution mandated that "all useful learning shall be duly encouraged and promoted in one or more universities"[50] and its Constitution of 1790 stated that "[T]he arts and sciences shall be promoted in one or more seminaries of learning."[51] But the conventions of both 1837 and 1873 rejected similar provisions. The delegates to these nineteenth-century conventions appeared to look upon higher education as a source of societal discontent and perhaps as a frivolity not worthy of public attention. For example:

> by my understanding Education in Pennsylvania is for all—for the mass of children. [Fostering arts and sciences] would lead to a grand State college, in the benefits of which the mass of our children can never participate.[52]

The apparent belief in both of these conventions that public education was meant to serve the masses may have contributed to the view that proper government policy should exclude the relatively small population composed of handicapped children.

The Public and Education

Descriptions in several communications of the Bureau of Education implied that though designated as "public," the education of handicapped children differed from that of the ablebodied majority. The beginnings of public education for handicapped children may have created that difference by adding onto the stereotype derived from traditions of devaluation and segregation. This final section will point out some of the components of this differentiating, and therefore disabling, process.

Perhaps as a consequence of Progressive ideology, 1899 marked a profound change in the official relationship between government and physically handicapped children. Giving aid to privately structured schools apparently was no longer thought to be an adequate expression of public duty and the state began to *initiate* their education. The City of Chicago established the first municipal public school for orthopedically impaired children in 1899.[53] According to an article by Solenberger, by 1918 six cities had developed similar schools[54] and several others had established special classrooms in "regular" public schools. Keesecker's "Digest of Legislation for Education of Crippled Children" notes the variations in the laws of the seventeen states which had established such institutions by 1929.[55]

The surveys by Solenberger (nee Reeves) of American institutions for physically handicapped children indicate that most orthopedic abnormalities had resulted from poliomyelitis, tuberculosis, or congenital defect.[56] She reports that medical attention was almost always necessary, and that schools were usually structured to provide for this need. For example, instruction was frequently given outdoors or in rooms with open windows, and periods of teaching were often flexible. Furthermore, a physician usually determined a child's eligibility for a special public school or special public classroom. In addition, the following statement by the Superintendent of the Chicago school suggests that administrators viewed the school as a kind of medical treatment: "The first aim of the school is to improve the physical condition of the children. The actual school work gives place always to this."[57] Even in these years, however, it is likely that not all handicapped children needed medical attention. But perhaps because their schooling was looked upon as a medical process, handicapped children were frequently considered to be sick. In this circular fashion, designating these children as patients and their education as a therapeutic measure both justified and engendered segregation. Furthermore, a "sick" label probably increased the uncertain behavior of those whom society already treated with the ambivalence reserved for people whose welfare depends on the generosity of others.

The custom of devaluating handicapped children probably was a general precursor of separate educational systems. The practice of devaluation, however, was almost surely strengthened by this medical basis, for the kind of thinking this rationale motivated produced a "scientific" (and therefore generally acceptable)[58] reason for segregation.

Another set of possible determinants of separate systems of education is suggested by comments made by Edith Reeves Solenberger in a *Bulletin* of the Bureau of Education. She begins her description of public school classes for handicapped children by making a strong case for integrated education:

> Every child wants to be like other children. The habit of children over 6 years of age is to go to school. Any child who is unable to do so because he is physically crippled misses a great deal more than instruction. Many crippled children have grown up to be "queer" in an unnecessary degree because they have mingled so little with children of their own age. They have been treated in special fashion by their parents, sometimes harshly in ignorant homes, but more often with a mistaken kindness which saved the "poor cripple" of the family all exertion and robbed him of the ambition to develop such powers of mind and body as he possessed. For such children there is no other tonic like the give-and-take of life in the schoolroom and on the playground.[59]

However, Solenberger does not follow her argument by considering methods that might bring about such a "tonic." Instead she looks at segregation as a condition that is usually necessary for the education of handicapped children: "The educational needs of many crippled children cannot be met in classes attended by children who are physically sound."[60] Solenberger qualifies her declaration with the word "many." At the time, and for many decades thereafter, however, *any* handicapped child could be kept out of an integrated class by the personal beliefs or wishes of school administrators. Moreover, the sequence of these paragraphs in Solenberger's article indicates that she saw the children rather than their needs as special—an assumption that furthered the tradition of collecting individual children with physical impairments into a single category. An apparently casual observation also points to this presupposition: "In some schools, where cripples buy food in the regular school lunchrooms used by all children in the building, the crippled children are served first."[61] With the claim that special physical needs require a special system of public education, Solenberger helped to develop an official classification of children with handicaps. This formalized stigma imposed the cultural likes and dislikes associated with that category upon each child with a physical impairment.

That such a predisposition also informed schemes for educating children with mental deficiencies, is one inference that may be drawn from Wallin's *Education of Handicapped Children.* The theoretical justification for differential education set forth in his book is based on the "demonstrable fact" that "children who exhibit certain well defined kinds and degrees of specific or generic differences require . . . special educational training. . . ."[62] As is well known, though, frequent errors plague any process of determining "specific or generic differences." The abundance of misdiagnoses that were (and are) possible suggests that the prescription of "special educational training" was not always or precisely related to special educational needs.

Sarason and Doris speak to this point in their discussion of the philosophy and practices of Binet:

> For Binet, special classes were not an end in themselves because he knew how their existence could be used, wittingly or unwittingly, to produce interplays of an adverse sort for individuals. Like the traditional concepts of intelligence, special classes existed in and were shaped by their surroundings; they did not have an independent existence.[63]

According to a view propounded by Steven Lilly in 1979,[64] the profession of Special Education often regards handicapped children as people who are special rather than as people whose education requires special accommodations. Evelyn Deno made a similar point in an earlier book when she wrote of the habit of defining children with physical handicaps as patients:

> The viewpoint must switch from the present fix on pathology, which points the accusing finger of cause at the child, to approaches which emphasize the fact that the problem is not in the child but in the mismatch which exists between the child's needs and the opportunities we make available to nurture his self-realization.[65]

When Deno goes on to argue that a medical emphasis keeps some of the problems of physically impaired children from remediation by educators, she articulates one of the most crucial elements of the disabling process:

> The emphasis in "defect" residing in the child tends to focus attention away from the external variables which educators might be in a position to do something about.[66]

These points are spelled out, and added to, in a book written with the passion of parents of a child labeled "handicapped." That book, *The Magic Feather*,[67] shows that the segregation and low expectations that seemed to characterize the public Special Education program of New York City frequently resulted in children being taught to fail.

Solenberger's understanding of the meaning of physical cure points out another disabling consequence of basing educational practices on a medical model:

> It is important that the curriculum in a class including such children should resemble as closely as possible that in regular public school classes in order that the temporarily crippled children may return to regular classes with as little break as possible in their school career.[68]

To be sure, devising a curriculum to accommodate children who are temporarily crippled is understandable. But conceiving of the return to "regular classes" as a sign of advancement almost certainly contributes to the imputed inferiority of children with permanent handicaps.

Even the phrase "special educational needs" is disabling, for it hides the fact, and thus precludes the view, that most physically handicapped children need only special methods for the *delivery* of education. "Delivery needs" of handicapped children clearly differ from those of ablebodied children. Solenberger writes of a variety of needs: transportation, special architectural arrangements, particular design of school-room furniture, an abundance of exercise equipment, and assistance by other persons. But rather than understanding those requirements as accommodations for physical defects, she seems to use these physical necessities to define the central characteristic of education for handicapped children. Except for the single paragraph praising integration, her article focuses on the differences of children with physical defects.

As other writers have done, Solenberger considered vocational training especially important for handicapped children:

> A school for cripples must have more than the ordinary amount
> of equipment and supplies for handwork ... looms for making
> rugs ... liberal provision for work with paper, yarn, raffia, and
> reed, and cloth for sewing classes.[69]

And as other writers, she permits the conclusion that handicapped adults
can fit only into a particular set of jobs.[70] In the appendix to her article,
Solenberger asserts: "Separate classes for cripples are possible only in fair-
sized cities. Not many towns with a population of less than 10,000 have
need of a special class for cripples."[71] The bulk of the appendix contains
several suggestions for teachers in small towns and rural areas who find
themselves with one or two handicapped children of school age. It implies
therefore that the education of small numbers of handicapped children
should depend on the discretion of the individual teacher. The education
of these children seems to have been defined as a public responsibility
only if enough existed to fill a special classroom. Apparently Solenberger
continued the tradition of thinking (or assuming) that educating handicapped children was not an unconditional obligation of society, for her
recommendations seem to have been meant for teachers whose kind hearts
led them to instruct these children.

By 1930, sixty-six cities had special schools and/or special classes for
handicapped children. Although the numbers had increased, Arch Heck's
description of 1918 suggests that the motives for educating handicapped
children were unchanged: "It is not only a matter of public philanthropy,
but of public economy that the crippled child receive as complete mental
and physical education as is possible...."[72]

Solenberger's report continues the stereotypy illustrated throughout the
chapter. Although variable in rationale, her positions seem to express the
view that educating handicapped children requires a complex of methods
that are engrafted on, rather than integrated into, the existing system of
educating ablebodied children. Her article thus confirms that the education of handicapped children was accorded the status of an afterthought.
When public perceptions of scarcity are invoked to explain why the community can not afford necessary accommodations, it seems very likely
that this casual and extrasystemic education of handicapped children can
be easily abandoned.

Notes

1. John Locke, *Some Thoughts Concerning Education*, p. 1.
2. Eduard Seguin's *Idiocy: and its Treatment by the Physiological Method*
reports that the first public schools for feeble-minded children were begun by the

Commonwealth of Massachusetts (p. 13) and the State of New York (pp. 12–13) in 1846; Robert Scott's *The Making of Blind Men: A Study of Adult Socialization* says that public schools for blind children were started by Massachusetts in 1828 (p. 122) and New York in 1831 (p. 123). These schools represent exceptions to the usual sequence in which private schools are followed by state assistance to existing private schools and finally by public schools.

3. Philadelphia, *Common Council Minutes; Indenture Records; Alms House Admissions Book; Alms House Daily Occurrence Dockets.*

4. U.S. Dept. of Commerce and Labor, Bureau of the Census, *Heads of Families of the First Census of the United States Taken in 1790: Pennsylvania,* p. 10.

5. E.g., Alan Abeson and Jeffrey Zettel, "The End of the Quiet Revolution: The Education for All Handicapped Children Act of 1975."

6. E.g., Darvin L. Miller and Marilee A. Miller, "The Education for All Handicapped Act: How Well Does it Accomplish its Goal of Promoting the Least Restrictive Environment for Education?"

7. U.S., *An Act to amend the Education of the Handicapped Act. . . .* (1975).

8. See generally: R. Freeman Butts, *A Cultural History of Education;* Lawrence A. Cremin, *The American Common School: An Historic Conception; American Education: The Colonial Experience, 1607–1783* and *American Education: The National Experience, 1783–1876;* Marcus W. Jernegan, *Laboring and Dependent Classes in Colonial America, 1607–1783.*

9. Commonwealth of Pennsylvania, *Constitution of 1790,* Art. VII, Sect. 1, in Francis Newton Thorpe, ed., *American Charters, Constitutions and Organic Laws: 1492–1908,* p. 3099.

10. Commonwealth of Pennsylvania, *Proceedings and Debates of The Convention to Propose Amendments to the Constitution . . . commenced at Harrisburg, May 2, 1837.* Mr. Ingersoll, Vol. V, p. 187.

11. Ibid., p. 189.

12. Gwilym Davis, "The Education of Crippled Children," p. 9.

13. Robert Coram, "Political Inquiries: To Which is Added A Plan for the General Establishment of Schools throughout the United States, p. 143.

14. Commonwealth of Pennsylvania, *Proceedings and Debates of the Convention [of] 1837.* Mr. Chandler, Vol. V, p. 195.

15. Ibid., Mr. Merrill, p. 199.

16. Ibid., Mr. Barnitz, Mr. Fleming, pp. 241–42.

17. Ibid., Vol. V, p. 183.

18. Ibid., Mr. Read, p. 333.

19. Ibid., Mr. Cox, p. 263.

20. Ibid., Mr. Smyth, p. 248.

21. Ibid., Mr. Porter, p. 208.

22. Gordon S. Wood, *The Creation of the American Republic, 1776–1787.*

23. Ibid., pp. 53–54.

24. Ibid., see esp. the chapters "The Whig Science of Politics" and "The American Science of Politics."

25. Commonwealth of Pennsylvania, *Debates of the Convention to Amend the Constitution, in session from Nov. 12, 1872 to Dec. 27, 1873,* Mr. Darlington, Vol. VII, p. 682.

26. Pennsylvania, *Plan and Frame of Government for the Commonwealth or State of Pennsylvania, 1776,* Art. VII, Sect. 44, in Thorpe, ed., p. 3091.

27. Commonwealth of Pennsylvania, *Constitution of 1873,* Art. X, Sect. 1, in Thorpe, ed., p. 3142.

28. Philadelphia, *Report of the Committee Appointed at a Town Meeting . . . ,* p. 9.

29. Arch O. Heck, "Education of Crippled Children," p. 4.

30. Commonwealth of Pennsylvania, *An Act to Create a Board of Public Charities.* Apr. 24, 1869.

31. Commonwealth of Pennsylvania Board of Public Charities, *Annual Report of 1871*, pp. xvii–xviii.

32. Commonwealth of Pennsylvania, *Debates of the Convention [of] 1873*, Mr. Darlington, Vol. II, p. 638.

33. Ibid.

34. Ibid.

35. Henry H. Kessler, *The Crippled and the Disabled*, pp. 57–58.

36. Commonwealth of Pennsylvania, *Debates of the Convention [of] 1873*, Mr. Cochran, Vol. II, p. 643.

37. Ibid., Mr. Smith, p. 639.

38. Ibid., Mr. Hanna, p. 641.

39. U.S., *Annual Report of 1870* of the Commissioner of Education to the Secretary of the Interior, p. 77.

40. Kessler, *The Crippled and the Disabled*, p. 59.

41. Ibid., p. 60.

42. Merle Frampton and Hugh Grant Rowell, *Education of the Handicapped.* Education of blind children: Vol. I, pp. 29–35; of deaf children: Vol. I, pp. 66–86; of feeble-minded children: Vol. I, pp. 179–82.

43. Commonwealth of Pennsylvania, *Debates of the Convention [of] 1873*, Mr. Wherry, Vol. VI, p. 42.

44. Ibid., p. 44.

45. Ibid., p. 43.

46. Ibid., Mr. Purman, p. 62.

47. Statement by Superintendent of Public Schools of Cleveland, Ohio, cited in Edith Reeves Solenberger, "Public School Classes for Crippled Children," p. 29.

48. David Rothman, *The Discovery of the Asylum: Social Order and Disorder in the New Republic.* Rothman's book demonstrates the thesis that American society practiced incarceration as a means of social control. The same argument might apply to segregation of handicapped people.

49. Commonwealth of Pennsylvania, *Debates of the Convention [of] 1873*, Mr. Mann, Vol. VI, p. 45.

50. Pennsylvania, *Plan or Frame of Government for the Commonwealth or State of Pennsylvania, 1776.* Art. VII, Sect. 44, in Thorpe, ed., Vol. V, p. 3091.

51. Commonwealth of Pennsylvania, *Constitution of 1790*, Art. VII, Sect. 2 in Thorpe, ed., Vol. V, p. 3099.

52. Commonwealth of Pennsylvania, *Debates of the Convention [of] 1873*, Mr. Mann, Vol. II, p. 465.

53. Ward W. Keesecker, "Digest of Legislation for Education of Crippled Children," p. 1.

54. Edith Reeves Solenberger, "Public School Classes for Crippled Children." The cities were Chicago, Cleveland, Baltimore, New York, Philadelphia, Detroit.

55. Keesecker, "Digest of Legislation," pp. 1–13.

56. Edith Reeves, *Care and Education of Crippled Children in the United States;* Solenberger, "Public School Classes," pp. 11, 12.

57. Statement from Superintendent of Chicago's Public School for Crippled Children, cited in Solenberger, "Public School Classes," p. 22.

58. Richard Hofstadter, *Social Darwinism in American Thought*, pp. 5, 31–32. Hofstadter writes of the appeal of science that prevailed in America during the late 1900s.

59. Solenberger, "Public School Classes," p. 7. In the same paragraph that

argues for the need for social interaction, Solenberger relates disability to the individual psychological mechanisms that are implicit in the phrase "robbed of ambition." As this book has proposed, understanding disability as a remediable entity requires a broader focus, for at least some portion of the handicapped individual's behavior represents responses to socially denied opportunities.

60. Ibid.
61. Ibid., p. 17.
62. J. E. Wallace Wallin, *The Education of Handicapped Children,* p. 91.
63. Seymour B. Sarason and John Doris, *Educational Handicap, Public Policy and Social History: A Broadened Perspective on Mental Retardation,* p. 34.
64. M. Stephen Lilly, *Children with Exceptional Needs,* p. 17.
65. Evelyn Deno, "Special Education as Developmental Capital," p. 229.
66. Ibid., p. 232.
67. Lori and Bill Granger, *The Magic Feather: The Truth About "Special Education."*
68. Solenberger, "Public School Classes," p. 29.
69. Ibid., p. 15.
70. This is a basic argument of John Gliedman and William Roth in their report for The Carnegie Council for Children, *The Unexpected Minority: Handicapped Children in America.*
71. Solenberger, "Public School Classes," Appendix A, p. 48.
72. Heck, "Education of Crippled Children," p. 18.

CHAPTER 6

Conclusions: Policy Implications

This book has elaborated on the distinction between handicaps imposed by nature and handicaps conferred by social and political mechanisms. Except for acknowledging that remedying handicaps imposed by nature is in large part a matter of cultural variation, the subject of physical restoration has not been addressed. The major purpose of the concepts and empirical materials of this book has been to show that social policies help to create disability and social policies can help to erase it.

The method of historical analysis has disclosed a progressive interaction between legislation and the beliefs and opinions of society. One can thus see how particular legislative language can disable, how the disabling practices of segregation and sterotypy promote each other, and how charitable and educational institutions both transmit and generate disability. One can look at the growth of specific issues that continue to disable: measurement of human value by economic productivity, "medicalization," labeling of physically handicapped people as "special," and rejection of public responsibility.

Although the diverse materials of the book have been presented in separate chapters, each chapter has contributed to or drawn from a number of arguments. Such a fusion of materials and ideas characterized the focus on military pensions in Chapter 2. That chapter showed the legislative beginnings of the link between disability and the ethic of individualism, and of that between disability and poverty. It also provided some background for understanding how society has come to look upon disability as an intra-individual attribute, and how segregation and physical handicap have become so firmly associated.

Chapter 3 presented the case of injured workers. Their financial compensation, like that of wounded soldiers, depended on prior wage and degree of injury. Unlike soldiers, however, members of the "industrial

army" were deemed to be worthwhile citizens only if they were judged
to be "rehabilitatable." Even when handicapped civilians were trained to
become economically productive, their social opportunities were con-
stricted by the prevailing idea that they should be seen only in the work-
place.

American workmen's compensation legislation indicates a social reali-
zation that the problems caused by indusrtrial changes could not be dealt
with by customary law. While the legislation probably reflected the particular morality of the time, its fundamental theme appears unrelated to
the nation's "civil religion." For whether or not these laws expressed
collective beliefs in a sinful past, what they called disability was graded
strictly in terms of medical severity and without regard to possible societal
determinants. Perhaps because of the stabilizing (or stultifying) power of
legislative precedent, but perhaps also because of this concept of disability,
workmen's compensation seems to differ only in form from the early
government's maintenance of injured soldiers.

Moreover, the language of compensation laws should not have used the
term "disability" when what was meant is "an inability to be gainfully
employed because of injury." Such clarity in the early stages of developing
compensation law might have allowed the growth of beliefs that disability
is not merely a result of injury, but rather a complex construct dependent
upon personal attributes other than physical defect, and upon elements of
the social environment. This view of disability demands an ecological
perspective. Indeed, theory elaborated from an ecological paradigm
(rather than a medical paradigm) might have informed future government
policies and general social beliefs. Not only could the idea of social construction have been recognized, but practices also might have been developed to keep physical impairment from affecting civil status. In the
contexts discussed in Chapters 4 and 5, the same medical focus resulted
in disability being seen as a personal attribute, and a disabled person
being seen as a patient and an object of charity. Almost never were handicapped people allowed to be ordinary citizens.

Chapter 4 reviewed the beginnings of the federal response to handicapped people who are not gainfully employed. The disabling potency of
charity and of the theory of Social Darwinism were looked at in terms of
society's single-minded desire for economic productivity. The idea that
handicapped people are used to satisfy society's need for benevolent action
points to two major disabling mechanisms. First, the desires of society as
a whole almost inevitably enforce and reinforce conditions of dependency
upon handicapped people. From one viewpoint, the existence of a dependent, helpless group reflects society's need for a dependent, helpless group.

In another interpretation, suggested by Barry Adam's discussion of "inferiorization" and the preservation of dominance,[1] the practices associated with enforced dependency are used to control social order. The second disabling effect centers on the theory of Social Darwinism. When political conditions favor the practices related to that theory, people who have been valued only as charitable objects retain their value only if they can contribute to—or cease to be a drain on—the economic well-being of the nation.

Chapter 5 discussed the disabling effects advanced by three centuries of laws that have dealt with the education of handicapped children. Throughout the eighteenth century, local and state governments ignored children who were judged to lack the potential for contributing economically to society's welfare. Economically unproductive people were perceived not only as useless, but as morally and civilly deficient. Their education at best was seen as an expensive frivolity that could be justified only by the gratification it offered to a philanthropic society.

However, the number of publicly initiated attempts made to teach these children the skills necessary to support themselves accelerated during the nineteenth and early twentieth centuries. Although laws of the late twentieth century mandate the education of all children without regard to their economic potential,[2] children with handicaps are still seen as special and different from normal. To the degree that they are thus distinguished from ablebodied children, handicapped children are disabled. When this "specialness" is looked at in terms of democratic political theory, it can be seen that education has failed to assure the social equality of handicapped children. When it is looked at in terms of child development theory, education can be seen as failing to teach these children the limits of free choice. This significant deficiency in public education helps to explain difficulties in the implementation of non-discrimination—the principle that has governed educational mandates since 1975.

Furthermore, the incorporation of charitable principles into public education has contributed to the formation of a group whose rights and interests are of little concern to society as a whole. The individuals in this group are seen as a threat to society, are sentenced to a lifelong childhood, are considered to be perpetual patients, and are looked upon as inevitable beneficiaries of public generosity. Many studies have demonstrated problems of lowered self-esteem in children so labeled, of limited expectations on the part of their teachers (and of the children themselves), and of stigmatization and devaluation by other children and adults.

Although there are no indisputable antecedents of the "disability legislation" of today, a number of recent government documents suggest that the conceptions that informed early laws also inform contemporary policy. For example, in 1966 the Social Security Administration estimated that the handicapped population consisted of 7–12 million non-institutionalized people of the ages of 18–64.[3] In 1971, however, the only members of this group who were classified as rehabilitated were the 291,000 persons who were gainfully employed.[4] Furthermore, testimony at a 1972 congressional hearing pointed out that the word "work" has almost always been used by government to mean "gainful employment":

> the only work that is truly recognized and honored . . . is competitive employment in the open labor market. . . . To my way of thinking there are innumerable kinds of work. . . . Work is the way the individual involves himself in the mainstream of society and develops a sense of productivity and independence. . . . Our society is responsible for developing the untapped human resource of its severely disabled citizens.[5]

This definition indicates what seems to be a continued devaluation of the nonworker, and an unchanged concept of government obligation.

An example of the endurance of the idea of "disability as personal defect" can be seen in the findings of a 1979 United States Supreme Court case. The case, *Southeastern Community College v. Davis*,[6] was the first high court consideration of a dispute based on Section 504 of the Rehabilitation Act of 1973.[7] Davis was rejected for nurse's training at the college because her hearing was so impaired as to require lip reading. She brought suit against the school, claiming discrimination under the language of section 504:

> No otherwise qualified handicapped individual in the United States . . . shall, solely by reason of . . . handicap, be excluded from the participation in, be denied the benefits of, or be subjected to discrimination under any program or activity receiving Federal financial assistance.[8]

The district court that had heard the case earlier had held that Davis's rejection was lawful because she could not safely perform either in her training program or in her proposed profession.[9] That court's finding was based on a listing of situations in which Davis's hearing impairment could endanger patients. Presumably because the members of the Supreme Court defined disability as a personal defect, the justices were unable to think

in terms of how *particular situations* could permit her to function satis-
factorily. The conclusion was upheld.

Another sign of the roots of modern legislation exists in the 1975 law
that mandates the integration of ablebodied and physically handicapped
children in public education. This "Education for All Handicapped Children Act"[10] can be an unambiguous legal support for the advocates of
children whose educational needs *require* special educational programs.
But this same law, because it can lead to the imposition of special programs on children who do not need special programs, can be a force for
segregation. In this regard, it is interesting to note that the law's promise
of "a free *appropriate* public education . . ."[11] can be as subjective in
implementation as the 1873 proposal for public education for "every child
with *sufficient* mental and physical ability."[12] [my emphasis]

Just as did the workmen's compensation statutes of decades earlier,
each law of the mid-twentieth century has clearly defined disability as a
function of medical impairment. This more recent legislation, however,
no longer defines disability in terms of employment. As seen in Chapter 4,
the testimony given Congress before the enactment of the first rehabilitation acts came mostly from people whose profession was to work for
handicapped people. In contrast, citizens of diverse backgrounds testified
prior to the enactment of the 1973 amendments.[13] Although this difference
in the breadth of testimony welcomed by Congress may have had several
causal explanations, it supports an idea derived from the earlier reference
to Gordon Wood's description of the beginnings of political factions[14]:
the prevailing concept of disability is in some part a function of "who
decides."

This series of examples reflects assumptions that promoted institutionalized segregation. Obviously, segregation affects people with physical
handicaps and people with able bodies. People with physical impairments
are denied the social and civil opportunities available to people with able
bodies. What is more, they are treated (and may learn to think of themselves) as objects whose actions—in some instances, whose lives—are
permitted by the generosity of society as a whole. Both groups of people
may fail to learn tolerance for and respect for the great array of human
differences. Furthermore, the lives of both groups lack the enrichment
brought by diversity. A major consequence of a segregated educational
system is the fear that is fostered by ignorance. This kind of fear among
those empowered to construct educational policy almost certainly engen-
ders the justification of more segregation.

It may also be the case that segregation persists because of widespread
beliefs that integration for physically disabled persons is not a matter of

self-interest. To expect that ablebodied adults can learn to see their own interests in public treatment of physically disabled people seems silly and naive on its face—especially when many adults do not appear to see self-interest in favorable treatment of aged citizens. But the observations indicating that laws effect attitudinal change in adults, make well-thought-out legislation seem a reasonable, although decidedly partial, tactic for achieving integration. Probably the most certain method of accomplishing this democratic promise, however, depends on the structure and substance of education. Although the argument for relating education and integration is an old one, two studies that represent a large body of systematic research give it special validity in the case of handicapped people.

Research by Lehrer[15] found that ablebodied fourth-grade children who were "mainstreamed" developed a less stereotypic schema of handicap than did non-mainstreamed children. A set of experiments by Fish[16] indicated that a semester of fieldwork by college-age counseling students did not change their attitudes toward handicapped people. Juxtaposing these two studies suggests that the development of attitudes in young children is especially sensitive to an educational structure that appears to authorize a standard of physical difference. It seems reasonable to conclude that contact between age-mates in early developmental stages of life can *prevent* formation of the stereotypes that justify devaluation. Perhaps contact among children can also produce an identification with others that results in an awareness of the self-interest that may be a necessary precondition of integration.

This book has not focused on the prescription of public policies that deal with handicapped Americans. Its intentions are instead to demonstrate the many roots of the construct of disability that have grown from early legislation and public documents. It is hoped, however, that these investigations will contribute to the formulation of policies that permit handicapped people as much opportunity as ablebodied people to choose whether and how to enrich themselves and their communities. To that end, the following reflections are offered.

1. The more that the methods of dealing with handicapped people lack government support and are structured to depend upon various forms of private charitable actions, the more those people will be looked upon as inherently inferior.

2. The more that society considers handicapped people both entitled to social opportunities and obliged to perform the duties of other citizens, the more that they will *be* as other citizens.

3. The less that segregation is built into voting booths, educational

institutions, public transportation and sites for work and recreation, the fewer will be the inferences that translate biological defects into social defects.

4. The less that physical handicap is thought of in medical terms, and the less that the source of social deviation is thought to be within the physically abnormal person, the more attention can be paid to the socially created factors that force deviation.

5. The less that individual worth is measured by the ability to be economically productive, the less effective will be the dynamic of devaluating handicapped people.

6. The more that public education can focus on the interdependence of groups and individuals, and can thereby increase tolerance for differences, the more it will be seen that physical status is simply physical status, and that political equality is not a function of physical impairment.

Notes

1. Barry D. Adam, *The Survival of Domination.*
2. U.S., *An Act to amend the Education of the Handicapped Act . . . .* (1975).
3. Kathryn H. Allan and Mildred E. Cinsky, "General Characteristics of the Disabled Population," p. 25.
4. U.S. Dept. of Health, Education and Welfare, Social and Rehabilitation Services, Rehabilitation Services Administration, *State Vocational Rehabilitation Agency Program Data: F. Y. 1971.*
5. U.S. House Select Subcommittee on Education of the Committee on Education and Labor (92-2), *Hearings* on bills to amend the Vocational Rehabilitation Act. Held in Washington Jan. 31, Feb. 1, 2 and 3, 1972. Statement by Ernest Weinrich on behalf of the United Cerebral Palsy Association, p. 89.
6. *Southeastern Community College v. Frances B. Davis.* (1979).
7. U.S., *An Act to Replace the Vocational Rehabilitation Act . . . .* (1973).
8. Ibid., Sect. 504.
9. *Southeastern Community College v. Davis* (1976).
10. U.S., *An Act to amend the Education of the Handicapped Act.* (1975).
11. Ibid., Section 3(c).
12. Commonwealth of Pennsylvania, *Debates of the Convention to Amend the Constitution [of] 1873*, Mr. Darlington, Vol. VII, p. 682.
13. U.S. House Select Subcommittee on Education of the Committee on Education and Labor (92-2), *Hearings* on bills to amend the Vocational Rehabilitation Act.
14. Gordon S. Wood, *The Creation of the American Republic, 1776–1787.*
15. Ariella Lehrer, "The Effects of Mainstreaming on Stereotypic Conceptions of the Handicapped."
16. Joel H. Fish, "The Psychological Impact of Fieldwork Experiences and Cognitive Dissonance upon Attitude Change in a Human Relations Program."

BIBLIOGRAPHY

Books and Articles

Abeson, Alan and Jeffrey Zettel. "The End of the Quiet Revolution: The Education for All Handicapped Children Act of 1975." *Exceptional Children* 44 (1977–78), pp. 114–28.

Abt, Henry Howard. *The Care, Cure, and Education of the Crippled Child.* Elyria, Oh.: International Society for Crippled Children, 1924.

Adam, Barry D. *The Survival of Domination: Inferiorization and Everyday Life.* New York: Elsevier, 1978.

Allan, Kathryn H. and Mildred E. Cinsky. "General Characteristics of the Disabled Population." U.S. Social Security Administration, Office of Research and Statistics. Washington, D.C.: U.S. Government Printing Office, 1972.

Allport, Gordon W. *The Nature of Prejudice.* Garden City, N.Y.: Doubleday Anchor, 1958 (1st ed., Addison-Wesley, 1954).

Altmeyer, Arthur J. *The Formative Years of Social Security.* Madison: University of Wisconsin Press, 1966.

Ariès, Philippe. *Centuries of Childhood: A Social History of Family Life.* Translated by Robert Baldick. New York: Random House, 1962.

Athelstan, Gary T., ed. *The Disabled Worker: Overcoming the System's Barriers.* Proceedings of the Conference on the Disabled Worker. University of Minnesota, 1982.

Baker, F. M., R. J. Baker, and R. S. McDaniel. "Demoralizing Practices in Rehabilitation Facilities." *Rehabilitation Literature* 36 (1975), pp. 112–15.

Barnhart, Debra McCloskey. "The Dual Capacity Doctrine: Piercing the Exclusive Remedy of Workers' Compensation." *University of Pittsburgh Law Review* 43 (1982), pp. 3–14.

Bartel, Nettie, and Samuel Guskin. "A Handicap as a Social Phenomenon." Pp. 75–114 in *Psychology of Exceptional Children and Youth.* Edited by William Cruickshank. Englewood Cliffs, N.J.: Prentice-Hall, 1971. 3rd ed.

Bateson, William. "Biological Fact and the Structure of Society." *The Herbert Spencer Lecture.* Delivered February 28, 1912. Oxford: Clarendon, 1912.

Becker, Howard S., ed. *Outsiders: Studies in the Sociology of Deviance.* New York: Free Press, 1963.

———. *The Other Side: Perspectives on Deviance.* New York: Free Press, 1964.

Berger, Peter L. and Thomas Luckmann. *The Social Construction of Reality: A Treatise in the Sociology of Knowledge.* Garden City, N.Y.: Doubleday, 1966.

Berkowitz, Edward David. *Rehabilitation: The Federal Government's Response to Disability, 1935–54.* New York: Arno Press, 1980.

Berkowitz, Monroe, William G. Johnson and Edward H. Murphy. *Public Policy Toward Disability*. New York: Praeger, 1967.

Berkowitz, Monroe, ed. *Rehabilitating the Disabled Worker: A Platform for Action*. Report of the National Institute on Rehabilitation and Workmen's Compensation, University of Michigan, June, 1962. Washington, D.C.: U.S. Dept. of Health, Education and Welfare, 1963.

Bogdan, Robert and Douglas Biklen. "Handicapism." *Social Policy* (March/April 1977), pp. 14–19.

Bogdan, Robert and Steven J. Taylor. "The Judged, Not the Judges: An Insider's View of Mental Retardation." *American Psychologist* 31 (Jan. 1976), pp. 47–52.

———. *Inside Out: The Social Meaning of Mental Retardation*. Toronto: University of Toronto Press, 1982.

Boulding, Kenneth E. "The Boundaries of Social Policy." *Social Work* 12 (1967), pp. 3–11.

Bowen, Catherine Drinker. *Miracle at Philadelphia: The Story of the Constitutional Convention, May to September, 1787*. Boston: Little, Brown and Co., 1966.

Bromberg, Walter. *The Mind of Man*. New York: Harper, 1937.

Buckham, John W. *Progressive Religious Thought in America: A Survey of the Enlarging Pilgrim Faith*. Boston: Houghton Mifflin, 1919.

Buel, Richard, Jr. "Democracy and the American Revolution: A Frame of Reference." *William and Mary Quarterly* 21, Series 3 (1964), pp. 165–90.

Button, H. Warren and Eugene F. Provenzo, Jr. *History of Education and Culture in America*. Englewood Cliffs, N.J.: Prentice-Hall, 1983.

Butts, R. Freeman. *A Cultural History of Education*. New York: McGraw-Hill, 1947.

Chigier, E. and M. Chigier. "Attitudes to Disability of Children in the Multi-Cultural Society of Israel." *Journal of Health and Social Behavior* 9 (1968), pp. 310–17.

Clews, Elsie W. *Educational Legislation and Administration of the Colonial Governments*. New York: Macmillan, 1899.

Cobbett's *Parliamentary History of England*. London: Bagshaw, 1806.

Cohen, Albert. "Study of Social Disorganization and Deviant Behavior." Pp. 461–84 in *Sociology Today*. Edited by Robert K. Merton, Leonard Broom and Leonard S. Cottrell, Jr. New York: Basic Books, 1959.

Coll, Blanche D. *Perspectives in Public Welfare: A History*. Washington, D.C.: U.S. Dept. of Health, Education and Welfare, Social and Rehabilitation Service, 1973.

Collier, David and Richard E. Messick. "Prerequisites Versus Diffusion: Testing Alternative Explanations of Social Security Adoption." *American Political Science Review* LXIX (1975), pp. 1299–1315.

Conn, Herbert William. *Social Heredity and Social Evolution: The Other Side of Eugenics*. New York: Abingdon, 1914.

Coram, Robert. "Political Inquiries: To Which is Added A Plan for the General Establishment of Schools throughout the United States" (1791). Reprinted in *Essays on Education in the Early Republic*. Edited by Frederick Rudolph. Cambridge, Mass.: Harvard University Press, 1965.

Cremin, Lawrence A. *The American Common School: An Historic Conception.* New York: Teachers' College Bureau of Publications, 1951.

———. *American Education: The Colonial Experience, 1607–1783.* New York: Harper and Row, 1970.

———. *American Education: The National Experience, 1783–1876.* New York: Harper and Row, 1980.

Crick, Bernard. *In Defence of Politics.* Chicago: University of Chicago Press, 1972. 2nd ed. (1st ed., 1962).

Cruickshank, William, ed. *Psychology of Exceptional Children and Youth.* Englewood Cliffs, N.J.: Prentice-Hall, 1971.

Crunden, Robert M. *Ministers of Reform: The Progressives' Achievement in American Civilization, 1889–1920.* New York: Basic Books, 1982.

Crunk, W. A., Jr. "A Study of Attitudes Toward the Severely Disabled Among Five Rehabilitation Groups." *Dissertation Abstracts International* 36 (11-A) (1976), p. 7202.

Cubberley, Ellwood P. *Public Education in the United States.* Boston: Houghton Mifflin, 1919.

Daly, John. *Descriptive Inventory to the Archives of the City and County of Philadelphia.* Philadelphia: Department of Records of the City of Philadelphia, 1970.

Davenport, C. B. *Eugenics: The Science of Human Improvement by Better Breeding.* New York: Holt, 1910.

Davis, Gwilym. "The Education of Crippled Children." *American Journal of Care for Cripples* 1 (1914), pp. 5–13.

Decker, Leslie E. and Robert Seager, II, eds. *America's Major Wars: Crusaders, Critics, and Scholars.* Vol. 2: *1898–1972.* Reading, Mass.: Addison-Wesley, 1973.

De Jong, Gerben and Raymond Lifchez. "Physical Disability and Public Policy." *Scientific American* 248 (June 1983), pp. 40–49.

Dembo, Tamara. "Some Problems in Rehabilitation as Seen by a Lewinian." *Journal of Social Issues* 38 (1) (1982), pp. 131–39.

Dembo, Tamara; Gloria Ladieu Leviton and Beatrice A. Wright. "Adjustment to Misfortune: A Problem of Social Psychological Rehabilitation." Pp. 254–318 in *Blindness Research: The Expanding Frontiers.* Edited by Maxwell H. Goldberg. University Park, Pa.: Pennsylvania State University Press, 1964.

Deno, Evelyn. "Special Education as Developmental Capital." *Exceptional Children* 37 (1970), pp. 229–337.

Dentler, Robert A. and Kai Erikson. "The Functions of Deviance in Groups." *Social Problems* 7 (1959), pp. 98–107.

Des Jardins, Den. *Breaking Barriers With Cartoons.* Edmonton, Alberta: Alberta Handicapped Communications Society, 1982.

Dibner, Susan S. and Andrew S. Dibner. *Integration or Segregation for the Physically Handicapped Child?* Springfield, Ill.: Thomas, 1973.

Dixon, Robert Galloway. *Social Security Disability and Mass Justice.* New York: Praeger, 1973.

Eisenberg, Myron G., Cynthia Griggins and Richard J. Duval, eds. *Disabled People as Second-Class Citizens.* New York: Springer, 1982.

Elkind, Arnold B. "Should the Federal Employers' Liability Act be Abolished?" *Forum, American Bar Association* 17 (1982), pp. 415–21.

Faries, John Culbert. *Three Years of Work for Handicapped Men: A Report of the Activities of the Institute for Crippled and Disabled Men.* New York: The Institute, 1920.

Farber, Bernard. *Mental Retardation: Its Social Context and Consequences.* Boston: Houghton Mifflin, 1968.

Fiedler, Leslie A. *Freaks: Myths and Images of the Secret Self.* New York: Simon and Schuster, 1978.

Fish, Joel H. "The Psychological Impact of Fieldwork Experiences and Cognitive Dissonance upon Attitude Change in a Human Relations Program." *Dissertation Abstracts International* 42 (8-B) (1982), p. 3494.

Fordyce, Wilbert E. "Psychological Assessment and Management," in *Handbook of Physical Medicine and Rehabilitation.* Edited by Frank H. Krusen. Philadelphia: Saunders, 1965.

Frampton, Merle and Hugh Grant Rowell. *Education of the Handicapped.* Vol. I, *History,* Vol. II, *Problems.* Yonkers-on-Hudson, N.Y.: World, 1938, 1940.

Freedman, Jonathan L. and Anthony N. Doob. *Deviancy: The Psychology of Being Different.* New York: Academic Press, 1968.

Friedman, John Block. *The Monstrous Races in Medieval Art and Thought.* Cambridge, Mass.: Harvard University Press, 1981.

Friedson, Eliot. "Disability as Social Deviance." Pp. 71–99 in *Sociology and Rehabilitation.* Edited by Marvin Sussman. Washington, D.C.: American Sociological Association and U.S. Vocational Education Administration, 1965.

Galton, Francis. *Hereditary Genius.* London: Macmillan, 1869.

Garber, Lee O. and Newton Edwards. *The Public School in Our Governmental Structure.* Danville, Ill.: Interstate Printers and Publishers, 1962.

Gaylin, Willard, ed. *Doing Good: The Limits of Benevolence.* New York: Pantheon, 1981.

Gellman, W. "Roots of Prejudice Against the Handicapped." *Journal of Rehabilitation* 25 (1959), pp. 4–6.

Gilbert, Neil and Harry Specht. *Dimensions of Social Work Policy.* Englewood Cliffs, N.J.: Prentice-Hall, 1974.

Gillin, John Lewis. *Poverty and Dependency: Their Relief and Prevention.* New York: Appleton-Century, 1937.

Glasson, William H. "History of Military Pension Legislation in the United States." *Columbia University Studies in History, Economics and Public Law* XII (3) (1900), pp. 1–130.

Gliedman, John, and William Roth for the Carnegie Council on Children. *The Unexpected Minority: Handicapped Children in America.* New York: Harcourt Brace Jovanovich, 1980.

Goffman, Erving. *Stigma: Notes on the Management of Spoiled Identity.* Englewood Cliffs, N.J.: Prentice-Hall, 1963.

Gold, Marc. *Did I Say That?: Articles and Commentary on The Try Another Way System.* Champaign, Ill.: Research Press, 1980.

Good, Harry G. *Benjamin Rush and His Services to American Education.* Berne, Ind.: Witness Press, 1918.

Goodman, Norman, et al. "Variant Reactions to Physical Disabilities." *American Sociological Review* 28 (1963), pp. 429–35.

Gordon, Gerald, Odin Anderson, Henry Brehm and Sue Marquis. *Disease, the Individual and Society.* Schenectady, N.Y.: New College/University Press, 1968.

Gove, Walter R., ed. *The Labeling of Deviance.* Beverly Hills, Calif.: Sage, 1980.

Granger, Lori and Bill. *The Magic Feather: The Truth About "Special Education."* New York: E. P. Dutton, 1986.

Greer, Colin. "Public Schools: The Myth of the Melting Pot." *Saturday Review* (November 15, 1969), pp. 84–86, 102.

Haber, Lawrence D. "Identifying the Disabled: Concepts and Methods in the Measurement of Disability." *Social Security Bulletin* 30 (1967), pp. 17–34.

Haller, Mark. *Eugenics: Hereditarian Attitudes and American Thought.* New Brunswick, N.J.: Rutgers University Press, 1963.

Hanes, David G. *The First British Workmen's Compensation Act, 1897.* New Haven, Conn.: Yale University Press, 1968.

Hanks, J. R. and L. M. Hanks. "The Physically Handicapped in Certain Non-Occidental Societies." *Journal of Social Issues* 4 (1948), pp. 11–20.

Hansen, Allen Oscar. *Liberalism and American Education in the Eighteenth Century.* New York: Macmillan, 1926.

Haring, Norris G. and Richard L. Schiefelbusch, eds. *Teaching Special Children.* New York: McGraw-Hill, 1976.

Heck, Arch O. "Education of Crippled Children." U.S. Dept. of Interior, Office of Education, *Bulletin* no. 11. Washington, D.C.: U.S. Government Printing Office, 1930.

Heffner, William Clinton. *History of Poor Relief Legislation in Pennsylvania, 1682–1913.* Cleona, Pa.: Holzapfel, 1913.

Herde, Eugene W. "FELA—Should it be Abolished?" *Forum, American Bar Association* 17 (1982), pp. 407–17.

Hicks, John D. *Republican Ascendancy: 1921–1933.* New York: Harper and Row, 1960.

Hofstadter, Richard. *Social Darwinism in American Thought.* Boston: Beacon, 1955 (1st ed. 1944).

————, ed. *The Progressive Movement: 1900–1915.* Englewood Cliffs, N.J.: Prentice-Hall, 1963.

————. *The Age of Reform: From Bryan to F.D.R..* New York: Knopf, 1974. (1st ed., 1955)

Howards, Irving, Henry P. Brehm and Saad Z. Nagi. *Disability: From Social Problem to Federal Program.* New York: Praeger, 1980.

Howe, Samuel G. "The Causes and Prevention of Idiocy." *Mass. Quarterly Review* 3 (June 1848).

James, Marquis. "A Debt of Honor Paid with a Worthless Check." *American Legion Weekly* (September 19, 1919), pp. 1–3, 22, 28.

————. "A Pledge that Must Be Redeemed." *American Legion Weekly* (September 26, 1919), pp. 10–11, 24, 28, 31.

Jaques, M., et al. "Cultural Attitudes Toward Disability: Denmark, Greece and the United States." *International Journal of Social Psychiatry* 16 (1970), pp. 54–62.

Jayne, Walter Addison. *The Healing Gods of Ancient Civilizations.* New Haven, Conn.: Yale University Press, 1925.

Jernegan, Marcus W. *Laboring and Dependent Classes in Colonial America, 1607–1783.* Chicago: University of Chicago Press, 1931.

Jervis, Robert. "Hypotheses on Misperception." *World Politics* 20 (1968), pp. 454–79.

Jordan, John E. *Attitudes Toward Education and Physically Disabled Persons in Eleven Nations.* East Lansing, Mich.: Michigan State University Press, 1968.

Katz, Irwin. *Stigma: A Social Psychological Analysis.* Hillsdale, N.J.: Earlbaum, 1981.

Katz, Michael B. *In the Shadow of the Poorhouse: A Social History of Welfare in America.* New York: Basic Books, 1986.

Keesecker, Ward W. "Digest of Legislation for Education of Crippled Children." U.S. Dept. of Interior, Bureau of Education *Bulletin* no. 5. Washington, D.C.: U.S. Government Printing Office, 1929.

Kessler, Henry H. *The Crippled and the Disabled.* New York: Columbia University Press, 1935.

Kleck, Robert. "Physical Stigma and Nonverbal Cues Emitted in Face-to-Face Interaction." *Human Relations* 21 (1968), pp. 19–28.

Kleck, Robert E. and A. Christopher Strenta. "Perceptions of the Impact of Negatively Valued Physical Characteristics on Social Interaction." *Journal of Personality and Social Psychology* 39 (1980), pp. 861–73.

Koch, R. and J. C. Dobson, eds. *The Mentally Retarded Child and His Family.* New York: Brunner/Mazel, 1971.

Kosa, John, and Irving Kenneth Zola, eds. *Poverty and Health.* Cambridge, Mass.: Harvard University Press, 1975.

Kriegel, L. "Uncle Tom and Tiny Tim: Some Reflections on the Cripple as Negro." *American Scholar* 38 (1969), pp. 412–30.

Krusen, Frank H., ed. *Handbook of Physical Medicine and Rehabilitation.* Philadelphia: Saunders, 1965.

Kugel, Robert and Wolf Wolfensberger, eds. *Changing Patterns in Residential Services for the Mentally Retarded.* Washington, D.C.: President's Committee on Mental Retardation, 1969.

Kugel, Robert and Ann Shearer, eds. *Changing Patterns in Residential Services for the Mentally Retarded.* Revised edition. Washington, D.C.: President's Committee on Mental Retardation, 1976.

Kutner, Nancy C. and Donna R. Brogan. "Disability Labeling vs. Rehabilitation Rhetoric for the Chronically Ill: A Case Study in Policy Contradictions." *Journal of Applied Behavioral Science* 21 (2) (1985), pp. 169–83.

Ladieu, Gloria, Dan Adler, and Tamara Dembo. "Studies in Adjustment to Visible Injuries: Social Acceptance of the Injured." *Journal of Social Issues* 4 (1948), pp. 55–61.

Ladieu, Gloria, Eugenia Hanfmann, and Tamara Dembo. "Studies in Adjustment to Visible Injuries: Evaluation of Help by the Injured." *Journal of Abnormal Psychology* 42 (1947), pp. 169–92.

Lane, Roger. *Violent Death in the City: Suicide, Accident and Murder in Nineteenth Century Philadelphia.* Cambridge, Mass.: Harvard University Press, 1979.

Lehrer, Ariella. "The Effects of Mainstreaming on Stereotypic Conceptions of the Handicapped." *Journal of Education Research* 77 (1983), pp. 94–99.

Lerner, M. J., D. T. Miller, and J. G. Holmes. "Deserving and the Emergence of Forms of Justice." In *Advances in Experimental Social Psychology,* Vol. 9. Edited by L. Berkowitz and E. Walster. New York: Academic Press, 1976.

Lerner, M. J. and C. H. Simmons. "Observer's Reaction to the 'Innocent Victim': Compassion or Rejection?" *Journal of Personality and Social Psychology* 4 (1966), pp. 203–10.

Levitan, Sar A. and Robert Taggart. *Jobs for the Disabled.* Baltimore: Johns Hopkins University Press, 1977.

Lilly, M. Stephen. *Children with Exceptional Needs.* New York: Holt, Rinehart and Winston, 1979.

Link, Arthur S. *Woodrow Wilson and the Progressive Era: 1910–1917.* New York: Harper and Row, 1954.

Little, R. M. "Economic and Social Significance of the Vocational Rehabilitation Program." Federal Board for Vocational Rehabilitation: *Bulletin 93 Civilian Rehabilitation Series 8.* Washington, D.C.: U.S. Government Printing Office, 1924.

Locke, John. *Some Thoughts Concerning Education.* (1692–93). Edited by R. H. Quick. Cambridge: University Press, 1880.

Lowenfeld, Berthold, ed. *The Visually Handicapped Child in School.* New York: Day, 1973.

MacDonald, Mary E. *Federal Grants for Vocational Rehabilitation.* Chicago: University of Chicago Press, 1944.

McMurtrie, Douglas C. "Notes on the Early History of Care for Cripples." *American Journal of Care for Cripples* 1 (1914), pp. 27–42.

———. "A Study of the Character and Present Status of Provision for Crippled Children in the United States." *American Journal of Care for Cripples* 2 (1916), pp. 24–38.

Malthus, Thomas Robert. *First Essay on Population.* London: Macmillan, 1926.

Martin, Edwin W. "A National Commitment to the Rights of the Individual— 1776 to 1976." *Exceptional Children* 43 (1976), pp. 132–35.

Matzen, John Mathiason. *State Constitutional Provisions for Education.* New York: Bureau of Publications, Teachers' College, Columbia University, 1931.

May, Henry F. *The Enlightenment in America.* New York: Oxford University Press, 1976.

Mercer, Jane R. "The Meaning of Mental Retardation." In *The Mentally Retarded Child and his Family.* Edited by R. Koch and J. C. Dobson. New York: Brunner/ Mazel, 1971.

———. *Labeling the Mentally Retarded.* Berkeley: University of California Press, 1973.

———. "A Policy Statement on Assessment Procedures and the Rights of Children." *Harvard Educational Review* 44 (1974), pp. 125–41.

Merton, Robert K. "Social Structure and Anomie." *American Sociological Review* 3 (1938), pp. 672–82.

———. "The Self-Fulfilling Prophecy." *The Antioch Review* 8 (1948), pp. 193– 210.

Meyer, Adolph. "The Problem of the State in the Care of the Insane." *American Journal of Insanity* LXV (1909), pp. 689–705.

Miller, Darvin L. and Marilee A. Miller. "The Education for All Handicapped Act: How Well Does it Accomplish its Goal of Promoting the Least Restrictive Environment for Education?" *DePaul Law Review* 28 (1979), pp. 321–50.

Mills, C. Wright. *The Sociological Imagination*. London: Oxford University Press, 1959.

Moore, Barrington. *Reflections on the Causes of Human Misery and upon Certain Proposals to Eliminate Them*. Boston: Beacon Press, 1972.

Mowry, George. *The Era of Theodore Roosevelt*. New York: Harper, 1958.

Mussen, P. H. and Roger G. Barker. "Attitudes Toward Cripples." *Journal of Abnormal and Social Psychology* 39 (1944), pp. 351–55.

Nagi, Saad Z. *Disability and Rehabilitation: Legal, Clinical, and Self-Concepts and Measurements*. Columbus: Ohio State University Press, 1969.

National Industrial Conference Board. *Workmen's Compensation Acts in the United States: The Legal Phase*. Research Report No. 1. April, 1917 (Revised August, 1919). Boston: National Industrial Conference Board, 1919.

New York Times. 17:7 (March 30, 1921); 19:1 (April 6, 1921); 17:1 (April 7, 1921).

Notestein, Wallace. *The English People on the Eve of Colonization: 1603–1630*. New York: Harper and Row, 1954.

Obermann, Carl E. *A History of Vocational Rehabilitation in America*. Minneapolis, Minn.: Denison, 1965.

Parliamentary History of England: 4 Elizabeth. Collected by Several Hands. London, 1751.

Parsons, Talcott. *The Social System*. New York: Free Press, 1951.

Pastore, N. *The Nature-Nurture Controversy*. New York: Columbia University Press, 1949.

Phillips, William and Janet Rosenberg, eds. *Social Scientists and the Physically Handicapped*. New York: Arno Press, 1980.

———. *The Origins of Modern Treatment and Education of Physically Handicapped Children*. New York: Arno Press, 1980.

Pickens, Donald K. *Eugenics and the Progressives*. Nashville, Tenn.: Vanderbilt University Press, 1968.

Pritchard, D. G. *Education and the Handicapped*. New York: Humanities Press, 1963.

Pruger, Robert. "Social Policy: Unilateral Transfer or Reciprocal Exchange." *Journal of Social Policy* 2 (1973), pp. 289–302.

Reeves, Edith. *Care and Education of Crippled Children in the United States*. Survey made for the Russell Sage Foundation. New York: Survey Associates, 1914.

Rhodes, J. E., 2nd. *Workmen's Compensation*. New York: Macmillan, 1917.

Richardson, Stephen A., et al. "Cultural Uniformity in Reaction to Physical Disability." *American Sociological Review* 26 (1961), pp. 241–47.

Riddle, S. S. "Rehabilitating the Worker When Accident Prevention Fails." *Annals, American Academy of Political and Social Science* 123 (January 1926), pp. 217–24.

Rimlinger, Gaston V. *Welfare Policy and Industrialization in Europe, America and Russia.* New York: Wiley, 1971.

Roeher, C. A. "Significance of Public Attitudes in the Rehabilitation of the Disabled." *Rehabilitation Literature* 22 (March 1961), pp. 66–72.

Roosevelt, Theodore. *The Works of Theodore Roosevelt.* Memorial edition. (24 vols.) Vol. XVII: *State Papers as Governor and President;* Vol. XIX: *Social Justice and Popular Rule: Papers, Speeches and Essays Relating to the Progressive Movement;* Vol. XX: *America and the World War: Fear God and Take Your Own Part.* New York: Scribners, 1925.

Ross, Edward A. *Seventy Years of It.* New York: Appleton-Century, 1936.

Rothman, David J. *The Discovery of the Asylum: Social Order and Disorder in the New Republic.* Boston: Little, Brown, 1971.

Rubin, Jeffrey. *Alternatives in Rehabilitating the Handicapped: A Policy Analysis.* New York: Human Sciences Press, 1982.

Rudolph, Frederick, ed. *Essays on Education in the Early Republic.* Cambridge, Mass.: Harvard University Press, 1965.

Rys, Vladimir. "The Sociology of Social Security." *International Social Security Review* 17 (1964), pp. 3–34.

———. "Comparative Studies of Social Security: Problems and Perspectives." *International Social Security Review* 7–8 (1966), pp. 242–68.

Safilos-Rothschild, Constantina. *The Sociology and Social Psychology of Disability and Rehabilitation.* New York: Random House, 1970.

Santa Clara Law Review. "History of Unequal Treatment: Handicapped People as a 'Suspect Class' under the Equal Protection Clause." *Santa Clara Law Review* 15 (1975), pp. 855–910.

Sarason, Seymour B. and John Doris. *Psychological Problems in Mental Deficiency.* New York: Harper and Row, 1969 (1st ed., 1949).

———. *Educational Handicap, Public Policy and Social History: A Broadened Perspective on Mental Retardation.* New York: Free Press, 1979.

Sarason, Seymour B., et al. *Psychology in Community Settings: Clinical, Educational, Vocational, Social Aspects.* New York: Wiley, 1966.

Schachter, S. "Deviation, Rejection, and Communication." *Journal of Abnormal and Social Psychology* 46 (1951), pp. 190–208.

Scheff, T. J. "Typification in the Diagnostic Practices of Rehabilitation Agencies." Pp. 139–47 in *Sociology and Rehabilitation.* Edited by Marvin Sussman. Washington, D.C.: American Sociological Association and U.S. Dept. of Health, Education, and Welfare, Vocational Rehabilitation Administration, 1966.

Schlesinger, Arthur M., Jr. *The Age of Roosevelt: The Crisis of the Old Order, 1919–1933.* Boston: Houghton Mifflin, 1957.

Schlozmann, Kay Lehman and Sydney Verba. *Injury to Insult: Unemployment, Class and Political Response.* Cambridge, Mass.: Harvard University Press, 1979.

Schroeder, Oliver C., Jr. "The Law Speaks: Disability and Legal Practice." Pp. 79–87 in *Disabled People as Second-Class Citizens.* Edited by Myron G. Eisenberg et al. New York: Springer, 1982.

Schulz, Gustav F. "The Cripple in Primitive Society." *American Journal of Care for Cripples* VIII (1920), pp. 335–46.

Schur, Edwin M. *Labeling Deviant Behavior: Its Sociological Implications.* New York: Harper and Row, 1971.

———. *Interpreting Deviance.* New York: Harper and Row, 1979.

———. *Labeling Women Deviant: Gender, Stigma and Social Control.* Philadelphia: Temple University Press, 1983.

Scott, Robert A. *The Making of Blind Men: A Study of Adult Socialization.* New York: Russell Sage Foundation, 1969.

Seguin, Eduard. *Idiocy: And its Treatment by the Physiological Method.* New York: Wm. Wood, 1866. Reprinted by Teachers' College, Columbia University, 1907.

Shearer, Ann. "The Handicapped Person." Pp. 345–53 in *Changing Patterns in Residential Services for the Mentally Retarded.* Edited by Robert Kugel and Ann Shearer. Revised edition. Washington, D.C.: President's Committee on Mental Retardation, 1976.

Sherman, P. Tecumsah. *Workmen's Compensation Law: Personal Injury by Accident Arising Out of and In the Course of The Employment.* New York: Workmen's Compensation Publicity Bureau, 1916.

Snyder, Charles McCool. *The Jacksonian Heritage: Pennsylvania Politics, 1833–1848.* Harrisburg: Pennsylvania Historical and Museum Commission, 1958.

Solenberger, Alice Willard. *One Thousand Homeless Men.* New York: Charities Publication Committee, 1911.

Solenberger, Edith Reeves. "Public School Classes for Crippled Children." U.S. Dept. of the Interior, Bureau of Education *Bulletin* no. 10. Washington, D.C.: U.S. Government Printing Office, 1918.

Somers, Herman Miles and Anne Ramsay Somers. *Workmen's Compensation: Prevention, Insurance, and Rehabilitation of Occupational Disability.* New York: John Wiley and Sons, 1954.

Sontag, Susan. *Illness as Metaphor.* New York: Farrar, Straus and Giroux, 1978.

Spencer, Herbert. *Political Institutions: Being Part V of the Principles of Sociology.* New York: Appleton, 1883.

———. *Social Statics; or The Conditions Essential to Human Happiness.* New York: Appleton, 1884 (1st ed., 1868).

Spiegel, Allen D., and Simon Podair. *Rehabilitating People with Disabilities into the Mainstream of Society.* Park Ridge, N.J.: Noyes, 1981.

Strenta, A. C. and R. E. Kleck. "Perceptions of Task Feedback: Investigating Kind Treatment of the Handicapped." *Personality and Social Psychology Bulletin* 8 (1982), pp. 706–11.

———. "Physical Disability and the Perception of Social Interaction: It's Not What You Look At But How You Look at It." *Personality and Social Psychology Bulletin* 10 (1984), pp. 279–88.

Sullivan, Oscar M. and Kenneth O. Snortum. *Disabled Persons: Their Education and Rehabilitation.* New York: Century, 1926 (reprint edition, New York: Arno Press, 1980).

Sumner, William Graham. *What Social Classes Owe To Each Other.* New York: Harper, 1883.

Sussman, Marvin B., ed. *Sociology and Rehabilitation.* Washington, D.C.: American Sociological Association and U.S. Dept. of Health, Education and Welfare, Vocational Rehabilitation Administration, 1966.

Szasz, Thomas S. "The Myth of Mental Illness." *American Psychologist* 15 (1960), pp. 113–18.

———. *The Myth of Mental Illness.* New York: Harper and Row, 1974 (1st ed., 1960).

Talbot, H. S. "A Concept of Rehabilitation." *Rehabilitation Literature* XII (1961), pp. 358–64.

Taylor, Wallace W., and Isabelle Wagner Taylor. *Special Education and Physically Handicapped Children in Western Europe.* New York: International Society for the Welfare of Cripples, 1960.

Temple Law Quarterly. An issue devoted to discussions of the legal rights of handicapped citizens and of pertinent judicial actions. 50, 4 (1977).

Tiedt, Sidney W. *The Role of the Federal Government in Education.* New York: Oxford University Press, 1966.

Trattner, Walter I. *From Poor Law to Welfare State.* New York: Collier, 1974.

Vail, David J. *Dehumanization and the Institutional Career.* Springfield, Ill.: Thomas, 1966.

VanderKolk, C. J. "Physiological Measures as a Means of Assessing Reactions to the Disabled." *New Outlook for the Blind* 70 (1976), pp. 101–03.

Vash, Carolyn L. *The Psychology of Disability.* New York: Springer, 1981.

Vieweg, William F. "Erosion of the Exclusive Remedy Doctrine Against the Employer." *Forum, American Bar Association* 17 (1982), pp. 422–34.

Walker, Jack L. "The Diffusion of Innovations Among the American States." *American Political Science Review* LXIII (1969), pp. 880–99.

Wallace, Shirley G. and Albert D. Anderson. "Imprisonment of Patients in the Course of Rehabilitation." *Archives of Physical Medicine and Rehabilitation* 59 (1978), pp. 424–29.

Wallin, J. E. Wallace. *The Education of Handicapped Children.* Boston: Houghton Mifflin, 1924.

Wan, Thomas T. H. "Correlates and Consequences of Severe Disabilities." *Journal of Occupational Medicine* 16 (1974), pp. 234–44.

Watkins, Gordon S. *An Introduction to the Study of Labor Problems.* New York: Crowell, 1922.

Watson, Frank D. *The Charity Organization Movement in the United States.* New York: Macmillan, 1922.

Watson, Frederick. *Civilization and the Cripple.* London: John Bale Sons and Daniclsson, 1930 (reprint edition, New York: Arno Press, 1980).

Wecter, Dixon. *When Johnny Comes Marching Home.* Cambridge, Mass.: Houghton Mifflin, 1944.

Weintraub, Frederick J. et al., eds. *Public Policy and the Education of Exceptional Children.* Reston, Va.: The Council for Exceptional Children, 1976.

Welter, Rush. *Popular Education and Democratic Thought in America.* New York: Columbia University Press, 1962.

Whetham, William Cecil Dampier and Catherine Durning Whetham. *An Introduction to Eugenics.* Cambridge: Bowes and Bowes, 1912.

White, Thomas Raeburn. *Commentaries on the Constitution of Pennsylvania.* Philadelphia: Johnson, 1907.

Wilding, N. and P. Laundy. *An Encyclopedia of Parliament.* London: Cassell, 1958.

Wolfensberger, Wolf. "The Origin and Nature of Our Institutional Models." Pp. 59–171b in *Changing Patterns in Residential Services for the Mentally Retarded*. Edited by Robert Kugel and Wolf Wolfensberger. Washington, D.C.: President's Committee on Mental Retardation, 1969.

———. *The Principle of Normalization in Human Services*. Toronto: National Institute on Mental Retardation, 1972.

———. "Social Role Valorization: A Proposed New Term for the Principle of Normalization." *Mental Retardation* 21 (1983), pp. 235–39.

———. "Social Role Valorization: A New Insight and a New Term for Normalization." *Australian Association for the Mentally Retarded Journal* 9 (1985), pp. 4–11.

Wood, Gordon S. *The Creation of the American Republic, 1776–1787*. Chapel Hill: University of North Carolina Press, 1969.

Wright, Beatrice A. *Physical Disability—A Psychosocial Approach*. New York: Harper and Row, 1983, 2nd ed. (1st ed., 1960).

Yuker, Harold E., and J. Richard Block. *Challenging Barriers to Change: Attitudes Toward the Disabled*. Albertson, N.Y. National Center on Employment of the Handicapped at Human Resources Center, 1979.

Zola, Irving Kenneth. *Missing Pieces: A Chronicle of Living With A Disability*. Philadelphia: Temple University Press, 1982.

Public Documents

Chamber of Commerce of the United States. *Analysis of Workmen's Compensation Laws*. Washington, D.C.: U.S. Government Printing Office, 1960.

Federal Board for Vocational Rehabilitation. *The Vocational Summary of the Federal Board for Vocational Education*. Washington, D.C.: U.S. Government Printing Office, September, 1919.

———. *Annual Reports to Congress*. Washington, D.C.: U.S. Government Printing Office, 1918–1921.

Force, Peter, ed. *American Archives: Consisting of a Collection of Papers, Debates, and Letters and Other Notices of Publick Affairs*. Fourth Series. *From the King's Message of March 7, 1774 to the Declaration of Independence by the United States in 1776*. Fifth Series, *From the Declaration of Independence, in 1776, to the Definitive Treaty of Peace with Great Britain in 1783*. Washington, D.C.: Clarke and Force, 1839–1853.

Ford, Worthington Chauncey, ed. *Journals of the Continental Congress: 1774–1789*. Edited from the original records in the Library of Congress. (34 vols.). Washington, D.C.: U.S. Government Printing Office, 1906–1937.

George, Staughton, Benjamin M. Nead and Thomas McCamant, eds. *Charter to William Penn and Laws of the Province of Pennsylvania Passed between the Years 1682 and 1700, Preceded by Duke of York's Laws in Force from the Year 1676 to the Year 1682, with an Appendix Containing Laws Relating to the Organization of the Provincial Courts and Historical Matter*. Harrisburg: State Printer, 1879.

Great Britain. *Statutes at Large from the First Year of King Edward the Fourth to the End of the Reign of Queen Elizabeth*. London: Charles Eyre, 1786.

Hening, William Waller, ed. *Statutes at Large of Virginia: 1619–1792.* (13 vols.). New York: Bartow, 1823.

Lowrie, Walter and Walter Franklin, eds. *American State Papers from the first Session of the First to the second Session of the Tenth Congress, inclusive.* (38 vols.). Washington, D.C.: Gales and Seaton, 1834.

Massachusetts Bay, Province of. *Acts and Resolves, public and private, of the Province of the Massachusetts Bay, 1692–1780.* Boston: Wright and Potter, 1869–1886.

Pennsylvania. *Statutes at Large of Pennsylvania, 1682–1801.* Harrisburg: State Printer, 1903.

———. *Statutes at Large of Pennsylvania, 1802–1809.* Harrisburg: State Printer, 1915.

———. *Laws of Pennsylvania.* Harrisburg: State Printer, 1810 to date.

Pennsylvania Board of Public Charities. *Annual Reports.* Harrisburg: State Printer, 1871–1883.

Pennsylvania, Commonwealth of. *Proceedings and Debates of the Convention to Propose Amendments to the Constitution: Commenced at Harrisburg, May 2, 1837.* (14 vols.). Harrisburg: Packer, Barrett and Parke, 1837–1839.

———. *Debates of the Convention to Amend the Constitution of Penna.; in session from November 12, 1872 to December 27, 1873.* (9 vols.). Harrisburg: Singerley, 1873.

Pennsylvania General Assembly House of Representatives. *Legislative Journal.* Harrisburg: State Printer, 1871–1883.

Philadelphia, City of. *Alms House Admissions Book:* 1785–1800.

———. *Alms House Daily Occurrence Docket:* 1789–1790.

———. *Common Council Minutes:* 1763–February 1776; 1789–1800.

———. *Indenture Records:* 1785–1800.

———. *Report of the Committee Appointed at a Town Meeting of the Citizens of the City and County of Philadelphia on the 23rd of July, 1827 to Consider the Subject of the Pauper System of the City and Districts, and to Report Remedies for its Defects.* Philadelphia: Clark and Raser, November 6, 1827. (Pamphlet 994, No. 6. American Philosophic Society).

Plymouth, Colony of. *Records.* Vol. XI: *Laws.* Boston: White, 1855–1861.

Thorpe, Francis Newton, ed. *American Charters, Constitutions and Organic Laws: 1492–1908.* Washington, D.C.: U.S. Government Printing Office, 1909.

U.S. *Collection of Papers Relative to Half-Pay and Commutation of Half-Pay Granted by Congress to the Officers of the Army.* Fish-Kill: Samuel Loudon, 1783.

U.S. *Congressional Record.* Washington, D.C.: U.S. Government Printing Office, 1873 to date.

U.S. The Constitution of the United States of America. Washington, D.C.: U.S. Government Printing Office, 1975.

U.S. *Secret Journals of the Congress of the Confederation.* (4 vols.). Vol. 1: *Domestick Affairs and the History of the Confederation.* Boston: Wait, 1821.

U.S. *Statutes at Large.* Boston: Little, Brown, 1861–1871; Washington, D.C.: U.S. Government Printing Office, 1872 to date.

U.S. Bureau of Education. *Annual Statement of the Commissioner of Education to the Secretary of the Interior.* Washington: n. p., 1870.

U.S. Congress. J. Res. 16, Jan. 20, 1914.

U.S. Congress Joint Committee on Education, Hearings concerning the bill proposing military vocational rehabilitation, H.R. 12212. (65-2). April 30, May 1 and May 2, 1918. Washington, D.C.: U.S. Government Printing Office, 1918.

U.S. Congressional Commission on National Aid to Vocational Education. *Report of Hearings*. H. Doc. 1004 pursuant to J. Res. 16. (63-2). Published June 1, 1914.

U.S. Continental Congress. *Journals of Congress: containing the proceedings from September 5, 1774 to November 3, 1788*. (13 vols.). Philadelphia: Folwell's Press, 1800–1801.

U.S. Dept. of Commerce and Labor. *Bulletin of the U.S. Bureau of Labor Statistics. Washington, D.C.: U.S. Government Printing Office. Bulletins nos. 45 (March 1903), 74 (January 1908) and 126 (December 1913) reprint a number of workmen's compensation laws.*

———. *Bureau of the Census. Heads of Families of the First Census of the United States Taken in 1790: Pennsylvania.* Washington, D.C.: U.S. Government Printing Office, 1908.

U.S. Dept. of Health, Education and Welfare, Social and Rehabilitation Services, Rehabilitation Services Administration. *State Vocational Rehabilitation Agency Program Data: F. Y. 1971.* Washington, D.C.: U.S. Government Printing Office, 1972.

U.S. Dept. of Labor. *Report of the National Commission on State Workmen's Compensation Laws.* Washington, D.C.: U.S. Government Printing Office, 1972.

U.S. House. H. Res. 315, Sept. 30, 1919.

———. H. Res. 495, Mar. 15, 1920.

———. H. Report 1105 pursuant to H. Res. 495. June 4, 1920.

U.S. House Committee on Education. *Analysis by Rep. Fess of Discussions Concerning Vocational Rehabilitation for Disabled Soldiers by the Secretaries of War, Navy, Commerce, and Labor, the Director of the Federal Board for Rehabilitation, and a Representative of the Surgeon General.* H. Report 597 to accompany H.R. 12212. (65-2). May 23, 1918.

———. H. Report 31 to accompany H.R. 5225, June 10, 1919.

U.S. House Committee on Education and Labor. *Oversight Hearings Before the Select Subcommittee on Education. part 2.* Held at Washington, D.C. Nov. 30 and Dec. 10, 1973. Washington, D.C.: U.S. Government Printing Office, 1974.

U.S. House Committee on Rules. Consideration of H. Res. 315 that the Federal Board for Vocational Education be Investigated as to its Efficiency. (66-1). Oct. 9, 1919. (From the microfilm holdings of the Library of the Commonwealth of Pennsylvania).

U.S. House Select Subcommittee on Education of the Committee of Education and Labor (92-2). *Hearings on Bills to Amend the Vocational Rehabilitation Act to Extend and Revise the Authorization of Grants to States for Vocational Rehabilitation Services and for Vocational Evaluation and Work Adjustment, To Authorize Grants for Rehabilitation Services to Those with Sensory Disabilities, and for Other Purposes.* Hearings held in Washington, D.C., Jan. 31, Feb. 1, 2, and 3, 1972. Washington, D.C.: U.S. Government Printing Office, 1972.

U.S. Office of the President. *Reorganization Plan No. 1. Part 2. Federal Security Agency.* Prepared by the President and transmitted to Congress (76-1) pursuant to the Reorganization Act of 1939.

———. *Public Papers of the Presidents: Richard Nixon, 1972.* Washington, D.C.: U.S. Government Printing Office, 1974.

———. *Public Papers of the Presidents: Gerald Ford, 1974.* Washington, D.C.: U.S. Government Printing Office, 1975.

U.S. Senate Committee on Education and Labor. Report 2 to accompany S. 1213, June 3, 1919.

Statutes

(listed chronologically)

Great Britain. *An Act for the Relief of the Poor.* (1601). *Statutes at Large from the Fifth Year of Edward IV to the End of the Reign of Queen Elizabeth.* London: Eyre, 1786. Vol. 2, pp. 685–88.

Colony of New Plymouth. *Laws enacted in the session of 1836. Records of the Colony of New Plymouth.* Boston: White, 1855–1861.

Colony of Virginia. *Act X, 1644. Statutes at Large of the Colony of Virginia.* Edited by William Walter Hening. New York: Bartow, 1823.

———. *Act I, 1674 or 1675.* Hening. Vol. 2, p. 331.

Province of the Massachusetts Bay. *An Act for Levying Souldiers, 1693. Acts and Resolves, public and private, of the Province of The Massachusetts Bay.* Vol. 1, *Acts passed at the session begun and held at Boston, November 8, 1693.* Boston: Wright and Potter, 1869.

Province of Pennsylvania. *An Act For the Better Provision for the Poor Within This Province and Territories.* (1700). *Pennsylvania Statutes at Large, 1682–1801.* Vol. II, p. 20.

———. *An Act for the Relief of the Poor.* (1705). *Pennsylvania Statutes at Large, 1682–1801.* Vol. II, pp. 251–54.

———. *An Act for Supplying some Defects in the Law for the Relief of the Poor.* (1718). *Pennsylvania Statutes at Large, 1682–1801.* Vol. III, pp. 221–25.

———. *An Act Laying a Duty on Foreigners and Irish Servants Imported into this Province.* (1729–30). *Pennsylvania Statutes at Large, 1682 1801.* Vol. IV, pp. 135–40.

———. *An Act Imposing a Duty on Persons Convicted of Heinous Crimes and to Prevent Poor and Impotent Persons Being Imported into the Province of Pennsylvania.* (1729–30). *Pennsylvania Statutes at Large, 1692–1801.* Vol. IV, pp. 164–71.

———. *An Act Imposing a Duty on Persons Convicted of Heinous Crimes Brought into this Province and Not Warranted by the Laws of Great Britain, and to Prevent Poor and Impotent Persons being Imported into the Same.* (1742–43). *Pennsylvania Statutes at Large, 1692–1801.* Vol. IV, pp. 360–70.

———. *An Act for Amending the Laws Relating to the Poor.* (1748–49). *Pennsylvania Statutes at Large.* Vol. V, pp. 79–87.

U.S. *An Act providing for the payment of the Invalid Pensioners.* (1789). 1 Stat. 95. Ch. XXIV.

———. *An act more effectively to provide for the National Defence by establishing an Uniform Militia.* (1792). 1 Stat. 271. Ch. XXXIII.

———. *An Act to Regulate the Claims to Invalid Pensions.* (1793). 1 Stat. 324. Ch. XVII.

———. *An Act Concerning Invalids.* (1794). 1 Stat. 392. Ch. LVII.

———. *An Act to provide for certain persons engaged in the land and naval service of the United States in the Revolutionary War.* (1818). 3 Stat. 410. Ch. XIX.

———. *An Act concerning invalid pensions.* (1819). 3 Stat. 526. Ch. XCIX.

———. *An Act granting half pay to widows or orphans whose husbands and fathers have died of wounds received in the military service of the United States, in certain cases, and for other purposes.* (1836). 5 Stat. 127. Ch. CCCLXII.

Commonwealth of Pennsylvania. *An Act to create a Board of Public Charities.* (1869). Act No. 66. *Laws of Pennsylvania,* p. 90.

U.S. "Federal Compensation Act of 1906": *An Act Relating to liability of common carriers in the District of Columbia and Territories and common carriers engaged in commerce between the States and between the States and foreign nations to their employees.* P. L. 59-219. 34 Stat. 232 Ch. 3073. (1906).

———. "Federal Compensation Act of 1908": *An Act Relating to the liability of common carriers by railroad to their employees in certain cases.* P. L. 60-100. 35 Stat. 65 (1908).

———. "War-Risk Insurance Act of 1914": *An Act to authorize the Establishment of a Bureau of War Risk Insurance in the Treasury Department.* P. L. 63-193. 38 Stat. 711 (1914).

Commonwealth of Pennsylvania. *AN ACT Defining the liability of an employer to pay damages for injuries received by an employe in the course of employment: establishing an elective schedule of compensation: and providing procedure for the determination of liability and compensation thereunder.* Act No. 338 (1915) *Laws of Pennsylvania,* p. 736.

U.S. "The Soldiers and Sailors Insurance Law of 1917": *An Act To amend an Act entitled "An Act to authorize the establishment of a Bureau of War-Risk Insurance in the Treasury Department," approved September second, nineteen hundred and fourteen.* P. L. 65-90. 40 Stat. 398 (1917).

———. "The Vocational Education Act of 1917": *An Act To provide for the promotion of vocational education: to provide for cooperation with the States in the promotion of such education in agriculture and the trades and industries: to provide for cooperation with the States in the preparation of teachers of vocational subjects; and to appropriate money and regulate its expenditure.* P. L. 64-347. 39 Stat. 929 (1917).

———. "Military Rehabilitation Act of 1918": *An Act to provide for vocational rehabilitation and return to civil employment of disabled persons discharged from the military or naval forces of the United States, and for other purposes.* P. L. 65-178. 40 Stat. 617 (1918).

———. *An Act To amend an Act entitled "An Act to provide for vocational rehabilitation and return to civil employment of disabled persons discharged from the military. . . ."* 41 Stat. 158. (July 11, 1919).

———. "Vocational Rehabilitation Act of 1920": *An Act to provide for the promotion of vocational rehabilitation of persons disabled in industry or otherwise and their return to civil employment.* P. L. 66-236. 41 Stat. 735. (1920).

————. "The Social Security Act of 1935": *An Act To provide for the general welfare by establishing a system of Federal old-age benefits, and by enabling the several States to make more adequate provision for aged persons, blind persons, dependent and crippled children, maternal and child welfare, public health, and the administration of their unemployment compensation laws; to establish a Social Security Board; to raise revenue; and for other purposes.* P. L. 74-271. 49 Stat. 620 (1935).

————. *An Act To provide for reorganizing agencies of the Government, and for other purposes.* P. L. 76-19. 53 Stat. 561 (1939).

————. "The Federal Employers Compensation Act Amendments of 1949": *An Act To amend the Act approved September 7, 1916 (Ch. 458, 39 Stat. 742), entitled "An Act to provide compensation for employees of the United States suffering injuries while in the performance of their duties, and for other purposes" as amended by extending coverage to civilian officers of the Untied States and by making benefits more realistic in terms of present wage rates, and for other purposes.* P. L. 81-357. 63 Stat. 854 (1949).

————. *AN ACT to amend title II of the Social Security Act to increase old-age and survivors insurance benefits, to preserve insurance rights of permanently and totally disabled individuals, and to increase the amount of earnings permitted without loss of benefits, and for other purposes.* P. L. 82-590, 66 Stat. 767, 1952.

————. "Education of the Handicapped Act of 1966": *An Act To strengthen and improve programs of assistance for elementary and secondary schools, and for other purposes.* P. L. 89-750. 80 Stat. 1191 (1966).

————. "Education of the Handicapped Act of 1970": *An Act to extend programs of assistance for elementary and secondary education, and for other purposes.* P. L. 91-230. 84 Stat. 121 (1970).

————. "The Rehabilitation Act of 1973": *An Act To replace the Vocational Rehabilitation Act, to extend and revise the authorization of grants to States for vocational rehabilitation services, with special emphasis on services to those with the most severe handicaps, to expand special Federal responsibilities and research and training programs with respect to handicapped individuals, to establish special responsibilities in the Secretary of Health, Education, and Welfare for coordination of all programs with respect to handicapped individuals within the Department of Health, Education, and Welfare, and for other purposes.* P. L. 93-112. 87 Stat. 355 (1973).

————. "The Urban Mass Transportation Act of 1964, as amended, 1974": *An Act to amend the Urban Mass Transportation Act of 1964 to permit financial assistance to be furnished under that Act for the acquisition of certain equipment which may be used for charter service in a manner which does not foreclose private operators from furnishing such service, and for other purposes.* P. L. 93-650. 89 Stat. 2-1 (1974).

————. "The Rehabilitation Act Amendments of 1974": *An Act To extend the authorizations of appropriations in the Rehabilitation Act of 1973 for one year, to transfer the Rehabilitation Services Administration to the Office of the Secretary of Health, Education, and Welfare, to make certain technical and clarifying amendments, and for other purposes; to amend the Randolph-Sheppard Act for the blind; to strengthen the program authorized thereunder; and to provide for the convening of a White House Conference on Handicapped Individuals.* P. L. 93-516. 88 Stat. 1617 (1974).

Commonwealth of Pennsylvania. *AN ACT Amending the act of June 2, 1915 (P. L. 736, No. 338) entitled, as amended, "An Act defining the liability of an employer to pay damages for injuries received by an employe in the course of employment; establishing an elective schedule of compensation; providing procedure for the determination of liability and compensation thereunder; and prescribing penalties," further defining "maximum weekly compensation payable" and "the maximum compensation payable per week"; making the act compulsory and providing for actions at law for damages for certain noncompliance; providing for extraterritorial coverage; changing the waiting period and payments in connection therewith, computation and distribution of certain compensation and agricultural labor coverage; and incorporating certain existing coverages with changes as to computation of compensation thereunder.* Act No. 263. P. L. 782 (1974).

U.S. "Education for all Handicapped Children Act of 1975": *An act To amend the Education of the Handicapped Act to provide educational assistance to all handicapped children, and for other purposes.* P. L. 94-142. 89 Stat. 773 (1975).

Case List

(listed chronologically)

Plessy v. Ferguson, 163 U.S. 537 (1896).

Franklin v. United Railways and Electric Co. of Baltimore, Court of Common Pleas of Baltimore, Maryland (1904).

Howard v. Ill. C. R. and *Brooks v. Southern P. Co.,* 207 U.S. 463 (1908).

Central R. of N.J. v. Colasurdo, 192 Fed. Rep. 901 2nd circ. (1911).

Erie R. Co. v. Welsh, 242 U.S. 303 (1911).

Phila., B'more and Wash. R. Co. v. Schubert, 224 U.S. 603 (1911).

Jeffrey Mfg. Co. v. Blagg, 235 U.S. 571 (1915).

New York Central R. Co. v. White, 243 U.S. 188 (1916).

Northern Pacific R. v. Meese, 239 U.S. 614 (1916).

Shanks v. Delaware L. and W. R. Co., 239 U.S. 556 (1916).

Hawkins v. Bleakly, 243 U.S. 210 (1917).

Mountain Timber Co. v. State of Washington, 243 U.S. 219 (1917).

Cudahy Packing Co. v. Parramore, 263 U.S. 418 (1923).

Southeastern Community College v. Davis, 424 F. Suppl. 1341, D.C.N.C. (1976).

Southeastern Commmunity College v. Frances B. Davis. 442 U.S. 379 (1979).

INDEX